MEDITERRANEAN
FRANCE

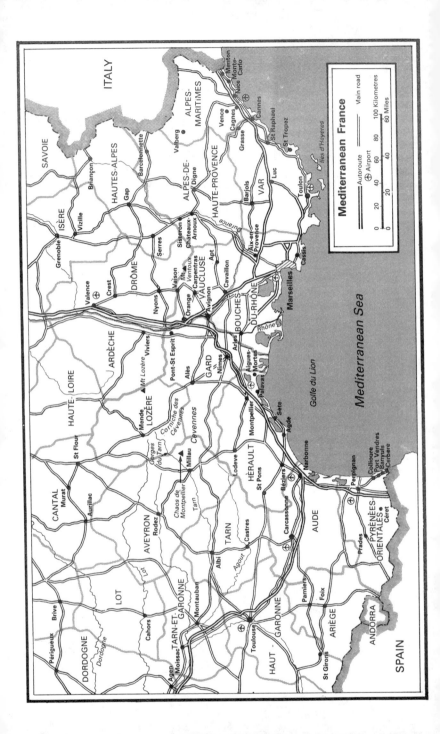

MEDITERRANEAN
FRANCE

The Thornton Cox
Guide

Maurice Rosenbaum
revised and expanded by
Mark Bryant & Ralph Cox

**THORNTON
COX**

Distribution:
Distributed in Great Britain and the Commonwealth by
Roger Lascelles, 47 York Road, Brentford, Middlesex TW8 OQP
Telephone: 01 847 0935

ISBN 0 902726 43 9

Distributed in the United States and Canada by
Hippocrene Books Inc., 171 Madison Avenue, New York NY 10016

US ISBN 0 87052 856 4

Published by Thornton Cox (I986) Ltd
4 Baches Street, London N1 6WB

Published in the United States and Canada by
Hippocrene Books Inc., 171 Madison Avenue, New York NY 10016

First published I975
Second edition I983
This edition, fully revised, March 1990

Original text by Maurice Rosenbaum
Additional material by Mark Bryant and Ralph Cox

Maps by Tom Stalker-Miller, MSIA
Drawings by Guy Magnus
Cover design by Eric Rose
Edited by Mark Bryant
Series Editor Kit Harding

Cover: Eze – Photograph by courtesy of the French Government Tourist Office
Photographs on pages 33 (bottom), 34 (top), 101 and 103 (top right) by courtesy of the
French Government Tourist Office; on pages 34 (bottom), 35 (top) and 36 by Mark
Bryant; all others by Ralph Cox

Typeset in 9 on 10pt Univers by
Goodfellow & Egan Phototypesetting Ltd, Cambridge, England
Printed and bound by The Guernsey Press Company Ltd, Guernsey, Channel Islands

---

Thornton Cox Guides:

Titles in this series include:

Egypt	**Kenya and Northern Tanzania**
Greece	**Majorca**
Ireland	**Portugal**
Southern Spain	**Southern Africa**

The Charterhouse of La Verne, Collobrières

Contents

Acknowledgements

The publishers would like to thank the French Government Tourist Office for their facilities and assistance during research work for this book. Valuable advice on Languedoc was also received from Rosalind and Michael Bowers and on Monaco by Ronald Payne. Many thanks to Françoise Jolly at the Regional Tourist Board in Marseilles and Marie Bersot in Nice.

Due to the original author's untimely death, this edition has been revised by Mark Bryant (Riviera and Côte d'Azur) and Ralph Cox (Languedoc and Roussillon).

Foreword

The holiday attractions of Mediterranean France are almost infinite; more than enough to appeal to most tastes in relaxation – physical exercise, exploration, sunbathing, or simply watching life in an unfamiliar setting flow round you in the morning sun.

It is a country made for such enjoyment, with outdoor café-terraces, village squares, great tracts of herb-scented *garrigue* or moorland, and mountains with almost impenetrable undergrowth and woodland – the *maquis* – to visit and explore. There are also ski-resorts within very convenient reach.

Then there are, of course, the so well-known delights of southern France: the food and wine, the shops and antiquities, the breathtaking survivors from a chequered past such as Carcassonne, the Château de Salses or the beautiful abbeys of the Pyrenees. Start with a conducted tour, by all means, to whet your appetite. Then go it alone and at leisure.

Throughout the South of France the quality of the light is remarkable; bright and luminescent, in combination with the richness and colours of the landscape it is prized by artists and visitors alike.

For wildlife and nature enthusiasts the region has much to offer, especially in the area at the mouth of the Rhône known as the Camargue. Lemon, orange, fig and olive trees, as well as a rich variety of wild herbs and flowers, thrive along the Mediterranean coast whilst the hinterland gives way to forests of pine and beech, vast areas of dry scrub, fertile valleys with vine-clad slopes and snow-capped mountains. In short, it is an area of contrasts full of never-ending delights for the visitor.

Do You Need to Speak French?

Obviously, you'll get more out of your holiday if you know some French: for one thing, you'll be able to explore further under your own steam and so discover out-of-the-way places and people who will go to endless trouble to show you the best of their own region. But a little French goes a long way, and you don't need an extensive vocabulary to explore the countryside within reach of your base, or to sit in a village café with a glass of wine or *pastis*, or to wander round the old towns on foot with a street map.

Inland Villages

Inland from the sun-baked beaches many villages are to be found perched in the hills and mountains: these hill-top villages are typical of Provence and, indeed, of the whole of the South. Some have already been prettified or transformed into a collection of tourist-trap boutiques, but many of them – many more than the unadventurous traveller may realize – are still unspoilt. They differ considerably in colour, character and remoteness, from the red sandstone, ochre and pantile clusters of the Languedoc and Roussillon, west of the Rhône Valley, to the golden-grey fast-nesses perched higher and more strongly walled in the hills to the east, near the Italian frontier.

In these villages are to be found those elements which entice the northern city-dweller: sun-warmed stone and plane-tree shade; olive groves and lemons; mimosa, oleander and bougainvillaea; lizards on low walls; small shops and street markets – not to mention the best climate in Europe.

They have, too, easy access to that marvellous coast and sea which, in the gaps between the busy resorts, is still one of the best holiday areas in the world.

Don't Write Off the Best Known Resorts

Don't make the mistake of writing off the Côte d'Azur and the Riviera because of what you have heard of the effects of package tours, over-building or pollution. Package tours give opportunities to get there cheaply but nobody is compelled to stay in a crowd. Pollution is, of course, a real problem, here as almost everywhere else in the seas of the world (nuclear and oil waste even where there is no serious quantity of human sewage), and the problem will have to be tackled before it is too late. But there are still stretches of unpolluted beach and sea between Marseilles and Menton (and even more between Marseilles and the Spanish frontier). Don't, therefore, allow yourself to miss any opportunity of seeing the colour and grandeur of the Esterel, the classical pine-clad coast of the Maures, and the lovely wooded capes and islands off the coast between Hyères and Menton.

The role played by the Mediterranean countries in world history must surely have some part in every European and American's consciousness, however little detailed history the traveller may have read. The past is certainly all around in the presence of the people, whose physique, looks and local dialects reflect their links with the ancient world of Greece and Rome, the Arab empires and the northern invaders. The historical flashbacks given in this book will, we hope, help to illuminate the walls of a castle or the alleyways of an old town for those whose knowledge of this or that dynasty, migration, battle, invasion or settlement is somewhat less than the learned scholar's.

What follows is, necessarily, a selection from the many places and resources of Mediterranean France. We hope it will encourage travellers to make their own explorations and discoveries.

General Information

Mediterranean France offers infinite scope for the independent traveller, whilst those who prefer to take an 'off the peg' holiday are well catered for by a variety of reliable tour operators. And planning your travel arrangements is certainly part of the fun of visiting this region.

Getting There By Air

The quickest route is, of course, by air; from London to Nice takes just under two hours and British Airways and Air France operate direct flights daily. Nice Airport (tel 93 83 03 00) handles Air Inter flights to and from numerous international destinations, including a daily direct service from New York. Marseilles Airport (tel 91 91 90 90) also operates internationally; both British Airways and Air France fly direct. Air France also makes regular flights from London to Toulouse Airport (tel 61 62 59 52).

Flying is expensive, but shop around to get the best deal: the regular return air fare from London to Nice is around £330, while it is possible to get a Fly-Drive package with Dan Air for under £200. For further information about flying to the South of France contact Air France at 158 New Bond Street, London W1Y 0AY (tel 01 499 9511), British Airways at 75 Regent Street, London SW1 (tel 01 897 4000) or the French Tourist Office.

Internal Flights
The South of France is well served by airports and in addition to those already mentioned you can fly to Perpignan (tel 68 61 22 24), Montpellier (tel 67 58 26 80), Nîmes (tel 66 20 12 40) and Toulon (tel 94 57 41 41), but normally only by transferring at Paris to pick up an Air Inter flight. Air Inter, the French internal airline system, operates an extensive network of routes throughout France and all airports serving the South have direct flights to Paris from where you can fly to almost any corner of the globe. Air Inter also offers worthwhile reductions on many flights, including international flights incorporating an Air Inter leg, as well as further reductions for students, young people under 26, pensioners, families (minimum three) and groups of ten or more. For full details write to Air Inter (Foreign Dept), 8 Rue Gauguet, 75014 Paris.

Fly-Drive
Dan Air (tel 01 930 5881, operates services from Aberdeen to
Toulouse, Gatwick to Perpignan, Montpellier and Toulouse and
from Newcastle to Toulouse. It is well worth investigating the
Fly-Drive fares Dan Air offers in conjunction with Europcar which
ensure the availability of a car on arrival and represent considerable savings on separate arrangements.

By Road

Driving Yourself
If time is not of the essence then a far more pleasurable way of
getting to the South of France from the UK is by car. The most
direct route is on the fast motorway (designated A – *autoroute*)
via Paris (A26, A1), Lyons (A6) and Avignon (A7), but there are
many alternative and more scenic routes using either the national
roads (designated N – *nationale*) or secondary roads (designated
D – *départementale*) including the traditional central route via
Paris, Moulins, Lyons and thence south following the *autoroute* –
but without paying the rather expensive tolls (toll routes are
clearly marked *péage*). If you are heading south-west, then it is
worth considering travelling via Rouen (avoiding Paris), Chartres,
Orléans, Limoges and Cahors. Allow two days or more for the trip
by car.

Route Maps
Before starting your journey a good road map is always a wise
investment, allowing you to plan the journey carefully in advance.
Geographia and Michelin publish good maps covering the whole
of France, and whilst buying your route-planning map consideration should be given to the more detailed local maps you
will need as well. Geographia produces good regional maps of
south-east and south-west France and for more details still the
IGN (the French equivalent of Ordnance Survey) *Cartes Tourist-
iques* 1:250,000 series, the Michelin 1:200,000 series and the
Recta Foldex regional maps at 1:250,000, are excellent touring
aids.

Documentation
When travelling by car remember that you will need a current
driving licence (minimum age 18), the vehicle registration book,
international third-party insurance (but preferably comprehensive and signified by a green card), a GB or nationality sticker and
a red triangle in case of breakdown.

General Information

Hints on Driving

Drive on the right and give priority to traffic coming from the right (*priorité à droite*). And remember to adjust your headlights for driving on the right; the French are accustomed to amber headlights and there is nothing more annoying to the French driver than to be dazzled by white, unadjusted lights! Two grades of petrol are normally available, *super* – high octane (4-star) – and *normale* (2-star). Speed limits in force are 60 kph (37 mph) in built-up areas, 110 kph (68 mph) on *routes nationales* and 130 kph (80 mph) on the *autoroutes*. Wear seatbelts if fitted and observe the rules – police who patrol roads and motorways (Garde Mobile) have powers to fine offenders on the spot.

The choice of route through France will tend to determine where you cross the Channel. The English Channel, apart from being the most crowded shipping route in the world, is also the most competitive – there are numerous crossing points and six major companies operating services:

Brittany Ferries:	Portsmouth – St Malo
	Plymouth – Roscoff
Hoverspeed:	Dover – Calais and Boulogne
	Ramsgate – Calais
P & O Ferries:	Dover – Boulogne
	Southampton – Le Havre
Sally Line:	Ramsgate – Dunkerque
Sealink:	Dover – Dunkerque, Calais and Boulogne
	Folkestone – Calais
	Newhaven – Dieppe
	Weymouth – Cherbourg
Townsend-Thoresen:	Dover – Calais
	Portsmouth – Le Havre and Cherbourg
	Southampton – Le Havre and Cherbourg

If you plan to take one of the westerly routes through France, a crossing to St Malo, Cherbourg, Le Havre or Dieppe could save you time. By hovercraft (Dover Priory station) France is just 40 minutes away with easy disembarkation on arrival. Tariffs resemble a jungle and vary with crossing, season, length of vehicle and so forth, although stiff competition for business has helped to hold fares at reasonable levels and off-peak and low season rates are available. Sally Line, a relative newcomer to the cross-Channel business, offers a simple tariff and attractive fares – a high-season return crossing inclusive of car (large size) and two adults costs around £210, and one child under 14 travels free.

By Coach
An increasingly popular and economical way of travelling to the South of France is by one of the regular coach services operating from London and selected points. Euroways, 52 Grosvenor Gardens, London SW1W 0AU (tel 01 730 8235) operates from London and Dover.

By Train

'Let the train take the strain' is a particularly useful idea if you are looking for a fast, pleasurable way to the South of France at prices to compete with the cheapest air fares. The train journey from London (Victoria) to Nice takes about 20 hours (less if you take the hovercraft across the Channel) and there are some excellent trains plying the route with couchette, sleeper and restaurant services (for example the luxury day train, the *Mistral,* and the *Train Bleu* which makes the journey overnight). Fast trains run from Paris to Toulouse, Montpellier and Marseilles and there is a comprehensive network of routes allowing access to most parts of the South by train. For the rail enthusiast there is also the exhilarating 162 mph (260 kph) TGV (*Train à Grande Vitesse*) running from Paris to Lyons in 2 hours 40 min.

Attractive fare bargains are available on French Railways, including a Holiday Return (*Séjour*) ticket which allows a 25 percent reduction on the ordinary fare for return journeys of over 1000 km (621 miles), Party tickets giving a 20 percent reduction for ten adults or more, the *France Vacances* card providing unlimited travel throughout the network at very reasonable rates and the *Carte Vermeil* for senior citizens with a reduction of 50 percent on the basic fare. For the under 26s an Inter-Rail ticket costing just over £150 entitles the holder to half-price travel in the UK, plus unlimited free travel in any of the 21 countries, including France, participating in the scheme.

Motorail
If you want your car in the South of France without the stress of driving it there then use the French Motorail service; put the car on the train at Calais or Boulogne for one of the Motorail terminals at Avignon, Narbonne, Nice or St Raphael, and relax. Alternatively you can pick up the Motorail service at Paris for these and other destinations. It is fast and comfortable, with a variety of good sleeping accommodation, but it's not cheap and you may miss some of the pleasant watering-holes to be dis-

General Information

covered on the drive down. For further information on travelling by rail consult your travel agent or French Railways, 179 Piccadilly, London W1V OBA (tel 01 493 9731).

It will be readily apparent from this brief survey that there are many ways of getting to the South of France, and in addition to making your own arrangements there are a great variety of inclusive tours available, incorporating many combinations of travel and accommodation, which any good travel agent will be able to advise you on. The French Tourist Office in London issues a useful booklet providing names and addresses of companies specializing in French holidays and travel.

Getting Around in France

Public transport in the South of France is generally excellent and there are good train services connecting the principal towns. Trains tend to run north-south and along the Mediterranean coast and in the high season are a sensible alternative to using the frequently overcrowded roads. Both private and public bus services will also get you to most destinations, and local tourist offices or *syndicats d'initiative* (referred to in the text either in full or abbreviated to SI) will supply routes and timetables on request. Scenic tours are available from terminals in Nice, Marseilles, Toulouse and most major tourist centres. Taxis operate in all towns and many villages, though you will have to phone for one. They normally have meters.

Car Hire
Car hire is normally no problem; there are agencies in all large towns and Hertz, Avis, Budget and Europ Car have offices at most airports. There are also numerous local hire companies offering competitive rates, but for peace of mind it is sensible to go for one of the known international companies. Check age limits – normally you need to be over 21 (in some cases over 23) and under 65 to hire a car. You must have a current driving licence held for at least one year. Weekly rates are more advantageous. Third-party insurance is usually included although it is well worth taking out full cover for a small additional fee. There is normally a deposit to find, although holders of major credit cards are exempt.

Bicycle Hire
Small motor bikes, motor scooters and ordinary pedal bicycles are widely available. Unless you pay by credit card you will be asked for a cash deposit.

14

Accommodation

From luxury hotels to small tents, a very wide range of accommodation is now available for the visitor to the South of France. Hotels are graded from 1- to 4-star plus a luxury category; you will not always find the word *hôtel* in the name, but *relais*, *residence*, *auberge* and *pension* are all equivalents, the latter being more like the English guesthouse. You normally pay for a double room without meals and costs will vary considerably depending on whether you stay at one of the popular coastal resorts or inland off the beaten track where living is still good and cheap. On the whole, hotels in the South represent very good value for money, and if the hotel has a restaurant it's usually worth trying out.

Self-catering

Self-catering is becoming increasingly popular in the region; villas, flats and houses are offered for rent either direct, or more usually, through tour or villa companies. If self-catering without the constraints of a package tour appeals, then the growing selection of *gîtes de France* is worth looking into – these are privately owned rural holiday homes partly financed by the French government, which sometimes also provide meals. Full information may be obtained from Gîtes de France, 178 Piccadilly, London W1V OPQ.

Caravanning and Camping

For the past decade or more the South of France has been successfully invaded by campers and caravanners, but more recently the business of hiring out caravans or tents on site as part of an inclusive package has come to the fore. However you arrange things, a good site is essential. In France caravan and camping sites are graded from 1- to 4-star depending on amenities, size of plots and the efficiency of site management. There is an enormous choice, so unless you enjoy crowds and noise it's best to avoid the very large sites where campers exist like sardines in depressing, if usually clean and efficient, uniformity. Some of the smaller sites, usually away from the coast, can be a delightful experience. Michelin and Letts publish guides to sites in France and, for the Mediterranean coast only, Roger Lascelles' guide lists over 120 useful sites. But bear in mind that experience counts for a lot when it comes to camping and caravanning, so if in doubt talk to someone who has done it!

A note of caution: the French pride themselves on the high standard of their campsites. But these accredited sites are in great

General Information

demand and it is essential, for the peak holiday periods, to make reservations in advance through the camping agencies, details of which can be obtained from French Government Tourist Offices. In some areas the behaviour of tourists who arrive without having booked places on sites is giving concern to the French authorities, both national and regional. Visitors who pitch tents wherever they find themselves, with disregard for local amenities or simple hygiene – and without seeking permission – make things difficult for all other campers.

More information about camping and caravanning may be had from the AA and RAC. The Caravan Club, East Grinstead House, East Grinstead, West Sussex RH19 1UA (tel 0342 26944) also runs a Foreign Touring Services department and the Camping and Caravanning Club, 11 Lower Grosvenor Place, London SW1W 0EY (tel 01 828 1012) is very useful.

Banking and Currency

Opinion is divided on whether it is best to take French currency, English travellers cheques or travellers cheques in French currency. For most holiday purposes a combination of currency and travellers cheques is advisable and if you purchase cheques in francs they tend to be easier to cash in smaller banks and other establishments and you will not be faced with the ups and downs in rates of exchange.

The prime unit of French currency is the franc (F), divided into 100 centimes: coins include 10, 20 and 50 centimes and notes 10, 20, 50, 100F. Like £sd in the UK, old monetary systems die hard so that people in France still sometimes refer to 'old francs' which disappeared over 30 years ago (100 old francs = 1 new franc).

Banks
Banks open 09.00–12.00 and 14.00–16.00 weekdays and are usually closed on Saturdays (sometimes Mondays). If you need to change money, make for a bank rather than a *bureau de change* as the rate of exchange tends to be lower; a hotel will often oblige but the rate will not be favourable. With a Eurocheque encashment card, available on application from most British banks, you can cash two cheques a day up to £50 each. The Midland Bank issues its own Eurocheques and Eurocards, with which larger amounts of money can be cashed. Big cities like Marseilles and Nice often have branches of NatWest, Barclays, American Express, etc, but in the smaller towns and villages of the South changing foreign money in any form can still pose problems.

Credit Cards

American Express, Visa (*Carte Bleue*), Access (Mastercard/ Eurocard) and Diners Club cards are accepted in most major hotels, restaurants and shops, especially along the Côte d'Azur, but in general you will not find it standard practice for the southern French to trade with plastic as it is in many other areas of Europe, and the USA in particular.

Climate

Allowing for variations in weather where hills and mountains cause sharper winters and higher rainfall, the South of France enjoys one of the most pleasant climates in Europe, with scorching summers and mild, dry winters. West of Toulon the coastal areas are affected by the cold mistral wind blowing down the Rhône Valley and the tramontane from the Pyrenees; the mistral is particularly aggressive in March but can rise quite suddenly at any time, even in summer.

In July and August the region is at its hottest (temperatures can often stay at 30°C around the clock) and the most crowded, although in Roussillon and Languedoc the weather is a little less predictable than on the Côte d'Azur. Spring and autumn are the rainy seasons, but the short, heavy showers are quickly replaced by idyllic spells of warm sunshine when the wild flowers and lush vegetation may be seen at their best. The average temperature at these times of the year is 17°C. Winters in the coastal South are usually mild (the temperature rarely falls below 10°C) and rainfall is slight, and it is no accident that the Riviera at this time of year became the refuge of Europe's aristocracy and royalty as early as the 18th century.

Customs and Immigration

A valid passport is essential. Visas are not normally required and there are no health requirements for visitors from the UK, Europe and North America. There are generous duty-free allowances on such items as cigarettes, wines and spirits and perfumes being brought into France, but do check since these change from time to time and vary slightly between imports from EC countries and other parts of the world; it is essential for UK visitors to know what restrictions apply for re-entry as the customs control on the return trip is likely to be more rigorous. Both countries are particularly vigilant against the transportation and use of drugs.

Festivals

The South of France is rich in musical, religious, cultural and sporting events throughout the year: the Monte Carlo Rally (January); the Nice Carnival (February); the Battle of Flowers at Vence (April); the Cannes Film Festival, Monaco Grand Prix and Grasse Rose Festival (May); the Festival of Sacred Music in Nice (June); the music festivals at Aix-en-Provence and Monaco (July and August); and the Menton International Chamber Music Festival are only the tip of the iceberg. For comprehensive information on all cultural events, there is a useful guide entitled *Festivals in France* available from French Tourist Offices.

Gratuities

Tipping for any service received is a way of life in France, but no one is going to get too ruffled if a visitor doesn't get it quite right. Restaurants and hotels normally add a service charge of 10–15 percent; sometimes your bill will state '*service non compris*' (service not included) in which case you will need to add the appropriate amount. At petrol stations it is customary to tip an attendant a few francs, depending on the service performed. A hotel porter will normally receive 5F per bag and a taxi driver 10–15 percent of the fare. But use discretion and tip according to the service you receive.

Medical Care

Health matters deserve attention when planning your trip. Fortunately, hospitals and medical care in the South of France are of a high standard and visitors from EC countries are normally covered under the French social security system which provides free hospital treatment and refunds about 80 percent of a GP's costs (you will have to wait a day or so for the refund whilst formalities are completed). However, it is generally wise to take out separate full medical cover for a worry-free trip. Should you require medical attention at any time it is best to start with the hotel reception which will normally put you in touch with a doctor. For minor ailments chemists (*pharmacies*), indicated by a green cross, are very helpful; the French pharmacist is trained more like a doctor for consultation on minor ills. *Pharmacies à garde*, or duty chemists, are listed in the local paper and their names and addresses are available from a police station or tourist office.

UK citizens can obtain full details of free medical protection in France in booklet SA36 available from any Social Security office;

you will need to complete form CM1 and will be given form E111 to take with you as evidence of entitlement to free medical treatment.

Tap water in the South of France is quite safe (except, of course, when marked *'eau non potable'* – not drinking water) even though mineral water might be the preferred drink; stomach upsets are normally caused by too much sun and an unaccustomed, often rich, diet – so start off with both in moderation.

Museums and Galleries

Opening hours of museums and galleries do vary, so check before you go. The norm is 10.00–12.00 and 14.00–17.00, although out of season opening hours are often shorter. They invariably close on Mondays. Admission is often free on Sundays.

The region is full of historical and artistic monuments and museums; churches and galleries abound and are not restricted to the major centres. Art lovers are particularly well catered for; from the medieval collection in the Palace of the Popes at Avignon to the many legacies of the Impressionists and their successors dotted around the Mediterranean coast, the range is extensive. You can see Paul Cézanne's studio at Aix-en-Provence, Picasso paintings at Antibes and drawings at Arles, Matisse paintings in Nice and a fine collection of modern art at Cagnes-sur-Mer.

Post Offices and Telephones

Post Offices are open weekdays 08.00–1200 and 14.30–19.00 and 08.00–12.00 on Saturdays. To telephone the UK, dial 19, wait for the continuous dialling tone and then dial 44 followed by your STD code but omitting the first 0 of the number. To telephone the USA dial 19 similarly, then 1 followed by the area code and number. Coin-box telephones mostly work internationally. Phone cards can be bought from most *tabacs* and give details of cheap rates etc.

Public Holidays

French national holidays are meticulously observed. They fall as follows: New Year's Day (1 January), Easter Monday (movable), Labour Day (1 May), VE Day (8 May), Ascension Day (movable), Whit Monday (movable), Bastille Day (14 July), Assumption Day

(15 August), All Saints Day (1 November), Remembrance Day (11 November) and Christmas Day (25 December).

Shopping

Shops, both large and small, offer an abundance of produce and merchandise, from the chic boutiques on the St Tropez waterfront to the village grocery store – and you can be sure of attentive and personal service. Supermarkets and the extension of this idea, the 'hypermarkets' – which incorporate shops of all descriptions and are springing up throughout the region – offer an extensive range of food and consumer goods of a surprisingly high quality. Provision shops are normally open 07.00–18.30/19.30, others open a little later at 08.30 or 09.00. In smaller towns and villages you will often find that shops close between 12.00 and 14.00 – siesta time, which is still a strongly observed custom in the South. A good number of shops close all day Monday.

If you are self-catering, experiment with the local produce – the quality and variety of cheeses, wines, fruit and *charcuterie* (processed meats) are excellent. Other good local buys include perfumes and soaps (Grasse is the centre of the French perfume industry), liqueurs, pottery, silk scarves and many articles carved in olivewood. For the more indulgent (and affluent), French tailoring and jewellery is displayed with tempting effect in the fine shops of Cannes, Nice and Monte Carlo. Local arts and crafts are well represented in the hundreds of small galleries throughout the South.

Sports

Watersports
The sea itself provides enormous scope for sporting activities, from a leisurely swim to scuba-diving, snorkelling, wind-surfing, sailing and water-skiing. There are good facilities for these sports everywhere, especially on the Côte d'Azur. Good beaches abound, with the exception of the area from the mouth of the Rhône to Marseilles. The open, sandy beaches of Roussillon are ideal for families with children, the only drawback being the narrow approach roads which tend to jam up in the high season. The coast between Marseilles and Toulon (Côte des Calanques) – an attractive stretch of steep limestone cliffs with many safe and sandy inlets – offers good resort and beach facilities, particularly at Bandol and Sanary. Further east along the Côte des Maures and the Esterel (with its pitted, red porphyry rocks), there are delightful beaches at Le Lavandou, St Tropez and St Raphael.

Unfortunately, pollution remains a problem, particularly on the Riviera coast, but at least it is recognized today and the authorities are working hard to repair the damage done over the past decades through industrial waste and untreated sewage. None the less, the Côte d'Azur is still one of the most polluted areas in the Mediterranean and you should take care to check the water if you swim away from the recognized beaches (earplugs are a wise precaution against infection).

Fishing, Golf, Skiing, Tennis
Although there is little chance of good sea-fishing, inland there are lakes, rivers and mountain streams to provide excellent sport for the angler (you will normally require a permit). Golf and tennis are popular and very well catered for, particularly around Cannes, Nice and Monte Carlo. For winter-sports enthusiasts there is good skiing in both the Alpes-Maritimes (Valberg, Beuil and Pra-Loup) and the Pyrenees (Mont Louis and Ax-les-Thermes). If you feel like entering into the spirit of things, try the local game of *boules*, a version of bowls. However, as a general rule, try and take any sports equipment with you as it tends to be expensive in France.

Tourist Offices and Consulates

Make as much use as possible of the many local tourist offices – *syndicats d'initiative* – which provide a very helpful service for the visitor, including free brochures, maps and hotel information. Principal offices on the coast are in Nice (Gare Centrale, Avenue Thiers) and in Marseilles (4 La Canebière).

Consulates
United Kingdom: 24 Avenue du Prado, 13006 Marseilles (tel 91 53 43 32)
USA: 9 Rue Armeny, 13006 Marseilles (tel 91 54 92 00) and at 1 Rue du Maréchal Joffre, 06000 Nice (tel 93 88 89 55).

Tourist Offices
Before you travel don't forget to pick up as much information as you can from the French Government Tourist Offices located in most capital cities, and at the following centres in the UK, USA and Canada:

United Kingdom: 178 Piccadilly, London W1V 0AL (tel 01 491 7622)
USA: 610 Fifth Avenue, New York NY 10020 (tel 212 757 1125)
Canada: 372 Bay Street, Suite 610, Toronto M5H 2WG (tel 416 361 1605)

Food and Wine

The South of France might well be described as a gourmet's melting-pot; although Provençal cooking is the predominant influence, Italian and Spanish dishes have blended successfully with the local cuisine to add great variety to menus throughout the region. Don't expect to find too much in the way of French classical cuisine, although it is served in some of the major restaurants and hotels.

The hallmarks of Provençal cookery are goodly quantities of garlic, olive oil, herbs, onions and tomatoes – although not always in that order and not as overpowering as the list might suggest: in fact, dishes *à la provençale* can often be subtle as well as exceptionally tasty. Soups are excellent – but usually filling. Try the local fish soup, *soupe de poissons*, made from finely ground small fish, garnished with grated cheese and served with *rouille* (a red sauce of Spanish peppers and garlic). *Soupe au pistou* is a thick vegetable soup topped with cheese and very satisfying.

Fish

The South of France is a paradise for lovers of fish, with plenty of fresh-water and sea varieties available. Particularly good and not too expensive are the *dorade* (sea bream), *loup de mer* (sea bass) and *rouget* (red mullet). Shellfish are usually imported. Lobster (*langouste – langoustine* is a smaller, but equally delicious type) is expensive everywhere, but Mediterranean prawns make a tasty and cheaper alternative. Many other fish delicacies abound in the small ports along the coast, where you can find mussels (*moules*) cooked in white wine, sea anemones (*violets*), Rhône eels and octopus. But the king of fish dishes in the South is surely the *bouillabaisse*, a fish stew crammed with an assortment of fish and shellfish; every town and restaurant has its own particular version, although Marseilles claims to be the place to eat it. But be warned, although undoubtedly an adventure worth the experience, *bouillabaisse* is a big meal requiring both appetite and patience!

Meat and Poultry

Meat and poultry are plentiful and frequently appetizingly prepared on charcoal grills or spit-roasts. Beef from the Camargue, often dubbed *boeuf gardien*, is worth keeping an eye open for. *Daubes* – or stews – are a feature of the region, served with noodles topped with sauce from the stockpot (*macaronade*). For the more adventurous there is *pieds et paquets* – a traditional Provençal dish of sheep's tripe stuffed with trotters, pork, garlic and onions simmered in white wine – or *alouettes sans têtes*, tender veal stuffed with cured ham, pork and herbs. *Saucissons* and sausages from Arles and Toulouse tend to have the edge on their British counterparts.

Fruit and Vegetables

The southern climate favours the cultivation of superb vegetables and fruit; melons, peaches, apricots, grapes and figs are plentiful and the enormous variety of vegetable dishes is an attractive feature of the cuisine. *Ratatouille* is a popular speciality made from a combination of tomatoes, onions, aubergines, courgettes and green peppers cooked in oil and, as a first course or light main meal, *salade niçoise,* which includes black olives, hard-boiled egg and tuna fish makes an appetizing dish. And the *assiette de crudités* or raw vegetable salad, is always reliable – try it with *aïoli*, a garlic-flavoured mayonnaise used as a dip. All sorts of snacks are popular with tourists and locals alike, including pizzas, *socca* (a kind of pancake from Nice), *tourtes* (savoury vegetable pastries) and *tian* (vegetable omelette); but remember that sandwiches are larger than life and made of long sections of French bread – *pain bagnats*, large round buns filled with fresh tomatoes, sliced onion, hard-boiled eggs and anchovies, are a tasty alternative, especially on the beach.

Don't neglect the tempting variety of rough country pâtés and the local cheeses, especially the drier ones made from goats' or sheep's milk (*de chèvres* or *de brebis*).

Wines

It is often the case that regional wines tend to complement the local food and the South of France is no exception: the southern French wines are generally light, dry and refreshing and you will be hard put to find a better accompaniment to the cuisine. Unfortunately, in the past the wines of the South have been overshadowed by the grander vintages of Bordeaux, Bourgogne and Beaujolais. But as these have become more and more expensive, growers in the South have put more energy into cultivating and expanding the vineyards of Provence, Languedoc-Roussillon and the Côtes du Rhône with encouraging results.

Food and Wine

The whites are generally dry and go well with local seafood dishes – Cassis and Palette are notable wines. Rosé wines from Provence and Tavel served chilled are light, refreshing and relatively cheap. Red wines are, however, more abundant and amongst them some excellent varieties are to be found: from Languedoc-Roussillon come Muscat, Minervois, Corbières, Fitou and Côtes du Roussillon. The best Provençal reds are Bandol and Palette, and the Rhône wines are numerous and good, although a little more expensive. Châteauneuf-du-Pape with its mellow, faintly aromatic taste is the most famous of the Rhône wines, but others from areas such as Gigondas and Lirac are well worth trying.

Les Antiques, St Rémy-de-Provence

The Culture and People of Mediterranean France

Provence

Provence has long been known as the land of the sun, even if this could hardly be true of every part of the region at all times. Van Gogh's sun and cypresses are the emblems; vine, olive and lemon the fruits. Warm honey-coloured stone and terracotta tiles characterize the buildings. The sun is always the key ingredient, whether illuminating the limestone ranges of Mont Ventoux and the foothills of the Alps, the mellow countryside of Aix, the

The Culture and People of Mediterranean France

austere solitude of the Camargue's lagoons, the *garrigues* of Nîmes or the interplay of land and water in the Rhône delta. Not for nothing has Provence attracted countless painters and poets to its colours.

The variety of the Provençal landscape is astonishing, from the harsh, sun-bleached rocks of the Lubéron to the rice-paddies of the Camargue, from alpine vegetation to market gardens, from sophisticated cities and beach resorts to primitive mountain villages. And integral to that landscape is the mistral, a cold wind which comes bellowing down the Rhône Valley like a bull, bursts over shipping off the coast with a crack like a gun, dries up the countryside in its path and can do real physical damage, quite apart from creating strange tensions and unease among some people. But the mistral's approach – and its departure after a few days – is marked by a crystalline clarity in the air, a pristine sharpness of detail in the distance, and a Tiepolo radiance in the sky as if the world has been washed clean.

The Heritage of Provence

With over 2000 years of civilization to boast of, Provence possesses both a rich legacy of arts and monuments and a thriving contemporary scene of festivals and exhibitions.

The Ligurians who lived here first left few traces: although they are the ancestors of Provence, their bloodlines mixed with Arab, Greek and Roman. Then Greek traders settled the coast, founding Marseilles and leaving an enduring influence, though not an architectural one. By contrast, reminders of Roman colonization are everywhere: the triumphal arch at Orange, the theatre at Arles and the great aqueduct of the Pont du Gard. Indeed the Roman province gave Provence its name. Christian influence arrived in the 4th century, to which many Romanesque churches bear tribute.

The Middle Ages to the Revolution

During the Dark Ages the Saracens laid waste the country, burning and pillaging far inland. Charlemagne gave Provence to his eldest son in 843. During the late Middle Ages it became part of the Kingdom of Burgundy and then of Arles. For several hundred years it was fought over by rival dynasties: constant conflicts of which castles like Rochemaure and the medieval walled towns of the southern Drôme are reminders. During the Great Schism of the Catholic Church (1337–1449) a rival Papacy to that of Rome was established at Avignon and the city remained the property of the Holy See until 1791. The region eventually emerged as an independent fiefdom, ruled by its own Counts from their capital of Aix. Among these was 'Good King René', who also introduced the muscat grape. Finally, Provence was united with France under Charles VIII, although it retained its own Parliament at Aix until the Revolution of 1789.

The Provençal Character
Out of this turbulent history was forged a Provençal character that is strong, fiercely independent and devoted to a multitude of local traditions, from the annual gypsy pilgrimage to the shrine of the Black Virgin at Les Saintes Maries-de-la-Mer or the procession of the Tarasque at Tarascon to the more modern Battle of Flowers at Nice.

Where is Provence?
Provence today is largely where you find it: and if this sounds unduly banal, remember that its boundaries have often shifted. The Hautes-Alpes of the modern administrative region were not in the Roman province. The Romans divided it into Upper and Lower Provence, with the capital at Aix, an area that included the modern departments of Alpes-de-Haute-Provence, Bouches-du-Rñone, part of the Drôme, the Var and the Vaucluse. Today the region of Provence-Alpes-Côte d'Azur is larger, extending east to Menton and the Italian frontier and north right up to Briançon and the Hautes-Alpes.
For our purposes, which are to cover areas easily accessible from the Mediterranean coast, we shall divide Provence into the Roman Provence of the Rhône Valley, alpine Provence between Grenoble and the Riviera, coastal Provence between Marseilles and St Raphael, and the Côte d'Azur with its mountain hinterland of the Alpes-Maritimes.

Routes Down to Provence
You can approach Provence from various directions by land. The most usual route is down the Rhône Valley via either the TGV train or the Autoroute du Sud. But equally there are two main routes into the region from Grenoble, via Sisteron or through Gap and Digne, the latter taking you through the Alpes-Maritimes to Grasse and Nice. These are dealt with in the chapter on alpine Provence.

Languedoc-Roussillon

Today, administratively, the country of the medieval troubadours' language – the *langue d'Oc* – is both smaller and larger than it used to be. It has lost the domains of the Counts of Toulouse to

The Culture and People of Mediterranean France

the west in what is now part of the Midi-Pyrénées. But it has gained Roussillon, the former fiefdom of the kings of Majorca, with its Catalan-influenced cultural background. This is why so many books disregard modern boundaries and include the Lot and Aveyron departments in Languedoc: it is why we treat Roussillon in a separate chapter.

Something of the character of Languedoc is given at the start of that chapter, while the complex history of Roussillon is explained in the descriptions of the two fortress cities of Carcassonne and Perpignan.

The famous bridge at Avignon

Provence of the Rhône Valley

The poet of Provence, Frédéric Mistral, took Pont Esprit as the gateway. 'It is there,' he wrote, 'that Provence makes its first appearance, where the bridge of St Esprit curves its 20 superb arches like a crown over the Rhône. It is the sacred portal, the gateway to the Land of Love. The olive, the proud pomegranate and the millet already adorn the slopes and their river valleys. The plain begins to widen, the woodland edge is green in the clear light, and the sky takes on the radiance of Paradise...' This is effectively where our Roman Provence begins, although we take in Montélimar a little further up the Rhône than Mistral would have approved.

Montélimar

Perhaps one of the most famous towns of Provence – for its stickily delicious nougat if nothing else – is Montélimar. With about 30,000 inhabitants, it is a well equipped holiday centre, with dozens of hotels and pensions, and plenty of opportunities for sport and recreation. It also makes a pleasant base from which to explore the Drôme to the east or the spectacular country of the Ardèche to the west. The SI is on the Promenade des Allées (tel 75 01 00 20).

Montélimar's name is a corruption of Mont Adhémar, the feudal fortress built here in the 12th century by the Adhémar family, whose last descendant, in the 17th century, was the Comte de Grignan, son-in-law of Mme de Sévigné. During the Wars of Religion Montélimar was beseiged and finally taken by the forces of the Reformation. Louis XIII gave the city to the Grimaldis, Princes of Monaco, who held it until the Revolution.

The Fortress
The fortress, which served as a prison between 1790 and 1929, is now open to the public except on Tuesday and Wednesday mornings. There is an admission fee. The ramparts give an almost 360-degree panorama with particularly fine views towards the Ardèche. The walk up to the south-east side of the fortress from the river takes one through the best of the old town which, as with many Provençal towns, is largely unspoilt (though it is also unrestored and gives a somewhat tumbledown impression).

Rochemaure Castle
A 6½ km (4 miles) drive along the D11 from Montélimar takes you to the ruins of Rochemaure Castle, across the Rhône from the city. Rochemaure ('black rock') is a hill on the right bank of the river where a basalt outcrop is in marked contrast to the neigh-bouring limestone scarps. It is capped by the ruins of the 13th-century fortress and its feudal walled village.

A further 5 km (3 miles) via Les Videaux and a 20-minute walk will take you to the Chenavri Peak with views past Rochemaure to the Rhône and surrounding hills.

Nougat
Nougat is the obvious local shopping speciality: street signs on the outskirts of the old town direct you to the many establish-ments where it is made. The key ingredients are almonds and honey.

Accommodation
The town's only 4-star hotel is Le Parc Chabaud (tel 75 01 65 66) with the Relais de L'Empereur (tel 75 01 29 00) running a close second. Among the less expensive ones, the 1-star Pierre on the Place des Clercs (tel 75 01 33 16) is clean and friendly with an attractive courtyard. It only closes in February but has no restaurant (there are numerous pleasant restaurants in the old town, notably Le Grillon in the Rue Cuiraterie). There is also a campsite close to town at the confluence of the Roubion and Jabron rivers.

Excursions into the Drôme
A strongly recommended diversion is eastwards from Montélimar along the Jabron Valley to the medieval towns of the southern Drôme. A round trip of 96 km (60 miles) by way of the D540 through La Bégude-de-Mazenc to Dieulefit, returning through Montjoux and Rousset to the D941 and then Valreas and Grignan, will give a tempting foretaste of what the Drôme has to offer. (Maps and guides to the area are available from the Syndicat d'Initiative in Montélimar.)

Dieulefit and La Bégude-de-Mazenc

Dieulefit, with its agreeable climate and beautiful surroundings, makes a pleasant place to stay. Hotels include the 3-star Les Hospitaliers (tel 75 46 22 32) which has an excellent restaurant. Campsites are also available. The town is known for its chinaware and pottery, both a particular feature of the Jabron Valley.

La Bégude-de-Mazenc, an old village now being rehabilitated, is built crowning a pine-capped bluff. You enter its narrow streets through a fortified gateway by the car park.

Grignan

Grignan, dominated by a Renaissance château, was the home of Mme de Grignan, the daughter of Mme de Sévigné. The town became famous through the letters written by Mme de Sévigné to her daughter whom she was nursing when she died in the castle. She is buried in its chapel. The castle, closed on Tuesday and Wednesday mornings, offers spectacular views from its terrace. An admission fee is charged.

You return to Montélimar by the D4, a wooded road running through the Citelles Valley and under the ruins of Rochefort-en-Valdaine castle.

South to Orange

From Montélimar the way south towards Orange offers the choice of using either the A7 *autoroute* (a *péage* over large stretches, which means that you pay a toll), or the old N7. Better still, take a combination of the departmental roads and the N7, exploiting the scenic advantages of going part of the way along the N86 on the west bank of the Rhône, through the spectacular Défilé de Donzère.

One recommended route is to leave Montélimar by the N102 towards Le Teil, turning off immediately after the canal on to the minor road (D237) that runs south between the Rhône itself and the canal that serves the Châteauneuf power station. After Châteauneuf-du-Rhône, as the cliffs close in, pick up the D73 to Viviers and the entrance to the Défilé de Donzère. Both the upstream and downstream bridges of the Défilé are best crossed on foot to appreciate the splendid views. The downstream one is reached via the N86, taking the D86J to the village of Donzère.

La Garde-Adhémar and the Val des Nymphes

Once back on the left or east bank of the Rhône pick up the D541 from Donzère and continue south, preferably breaking off to visit La Garde-Adhémar and the Val des Nymphes. La Garde-Adhémar has a fine Romanesque church, notable for its belfry and the freize in the west apse. Outside there is a good view west over the Rhône plain.

Val des Nymphes
Possibly once a place of pagan worship, the Val des Nymphes is now the site of a ruined 12th-century chapel lent enchantment by the sound of waterfalls.

Clansays and St Paul-Trois-Châteaux

A further 3 km (3 miles) detour to Clansays with its magnificent views is highly recommended. To reach it from Val des Nymphes continue along the D572A, turning right on to the D133 then left on to the D571. From Clansays you return to the D133 for St

Opposite:	*Palace of the Popes, Avignon (top right)*
	Back wall of the Roman Theatre, Orange (top left)
	The beach at Mourillon near Toulon (below)
Overleaf:	*Haute Clarée in the Hautes-Alpes (top)*
	The Public Gardens on Menton's seafront (below)

Paul-Trois-Châteaux: a misnomer since it is now and always has been without castles, although the old fortified town does boast an 11th-century cathedral built in the pure Provençal Roman-esque manner.

The Rhône Barrage and Rochegude

If you have time it is worth visiting the impressive Rhône *barrage* (dam) at Donzère-Mondragon, begun in I946 to provide electricity and irrigation and to improve navigation on the Rhône. Otherwise take the D59 to Suze-la-Rousse, then follow the D117, D11 and finally the N7 to Orange. The D117 passes through Rochegude, which has one of the best hotels in the area, the 4-star Château de Rochegude (tel 90 04 81 88). Elegantly sited and enjoying its own panorama of the Rhône plain, the Château offers excellent food as well as swimming and tennis.

Orange

Today the equivalent of a modest county capital with a popula-tion of 28,000, Orange grew during the early centuries of the Christian era from a Celtic settlement or township to become a Roman colony of such importance and prosperity that its popula-tion was far greater than it is today. The SI can be found on the corner of the Parc Gasparin and Cours A. Briand (tel 90 34 70 88).

Roman Orange

In the year 105 BC, Cymbrian and Teuton 'barbarians', whose physical stature in itself intimidated the smaller Romans, launched an attack with such success that 100,000 Romans were left dead. However, within three years the Roman general Marius inflicted an even more crushing defeat on the Germanic hordes before Aix, in a triumph which gave its name to the Montagne Ste Victoire: and also the name Marius to large number of Provençal boys, to say nothing of the great fictional Marseilles character in Marcel Pagnol's plays.

Dutch rule

A principality in the 13th century, Orange came, through marri-ages and inheritance, into the possession of a branch of the des

Previous page: *Pavement café in old Nice (top right)*
　　　　　　　　The Galleon in Marseilles harbour (top left)
　　　　　　　　Ste Marie Madeleine in the Ventoux (below)
Opposite:　　　*The Grand Casino, Monte Carlo (top)*
　　　　　　　　Menton harbour and town (below)

Provence of the Rhône Valley

Baux family and of the German principality of Nassau. In the 16th century William the Silent (William of Nassau, Prince of Orange) created the United Provinces, and the royal dynasty of Holland adopted the title of Orange. Thus the House of Orange-Nassau, while governing the Low Countries and, for a time, England, also cherished its tiny corner of France. Louis XIV, however, put a stop to all that and handed Orange over to the Comte de Grignan, son-in-law of Mme de Sévigné and Lieutenant-General of Provence.

The Commemorative Arch

If you enter Orange by the N7 you come almost immediately upon one of the city's two most impressive Roman monuments: the great commemorative or triumphal arch celebrating the exploits of Caesar's IIth Legion and its victory over the Massaliotes – the Greeks who had colonized Marseilles – in 49BC. The survivors of that Legion became the first colonists of Orange, then known as Arausio. The arch is one of the finest the Romans have left us anywhere.

The Théâtre Antique

The other magnificent memorial of the Romans is the exquisite and exceptionally well-preserved theatre – the finest example to be found in Provence, perhaps in the world. Situated on the other side of the city to the arch, the theatre was built during the Augustan era and still has its stage wall. Louis XVI called it 'the finest wall in the kingdom' – it is 103 m (338 ft) long by 38 m (125 ft) high – and only the roof and ornamental details are missing. Moreover, uniquely, the theatre still has its imperial statue of Augustus, albeit restored, saluting the spectators from the central alcove in the wall, above the stage.

Lapidary Museum

Admission to the theatre includes the Musée Lapidaire opposite. Here stonework excavated from the theatre is on display along with local artwork.

The Chorégies

The Chorégies, the opera festivals staged in the theatre at the end of July, are an unforgettable experience. Details are obtainable from the Maison des Chorégies, Place Sylvain (tel 90 34 15 22 or 90 34 24 24).

The Capitol

Adjoining the theatre are the remains of the Capitol and one of the three known gymnasiums. The rest of the Roman city has disappeared, much having been used to build the defensive system conceived by Maurice of Nassau in 1622. The arch and theatre were spared only by their incorporation into the defences.

St Eutrope Hill
Above the theatre are the open spaces of the Colline St Eutrope, the hill into which the auditorium was built. From it views embrace the theatre, the town and the mountains of the Dentelles de Montmirail as well as Mont Ventoux to the east.

Accommodation
Orange boasts numerous hotels. 3-star ones include the Arène (tel 90 34 10 95), situated in the quiet of the Place de Langes, though it has no restaurant, and the comfortable Louvre et Terminus (tel 90 34 10 08), found conveniently close to the railway station as its name suggests. Less expensive are the Hôtel le Français (tel 90 34 67 65), a well-kept establishment again close to the station in the Avenue Frédéric Mistral, the 1-star Hôtel des Arts (tel 90 34 01 88) and Le Fréau (tel 90 34 06 26). The Colline St Eutrope has both a campsite (tel 90 34 09 22) and an open-air swimming-pool.

Restaurants
Restaurants are equally numerous, of which La Pigraillet in Chemin Colline St Eutrope is the most notable. Le Forum, near the theatre, and Le Provençal at 27 Rue de la Republic, are good alternatives. For a midday snack there is always the traditional *pain bagnat*, a salad-filled sandwich that can be ordered in any of the many cafés and eaten at tables outside in the sun.

East of Orange/Mont Ventoux
Almost every route has attractive variants; instead of driving direct from Orange to Avignon, the N7 lacking any charm in this section, one might well – time, money, the volume of traffic and family tensions permitting – make a fairly extensive detour by the D975 to Vaison-la-Romaine and the Ventoux mountains.

Vaison-la-Romaine

A settlement since the Bronze Age, and later a capital of the Gauls, Vaison is nowadays one of the key sites for Roman antiquities in Provence. It is also an attractively situated medieval town and holiday resort, ideal for excursions into the Ventoux range or the Dentelles de Montmirail. The SI is in Place du Chanoine Santel (tel 90 36 02 11).

Provence of the Rhône Valley

The Romans arrived in 12BC and built Vaison into a wealthy residential centre as opposed to the more grandiose cities of Arles and Orange. The modern town arose both on top of the Roman remains (now partly excavated) and between them and the River Ouvèze, whose green waters are spanned by an attractive single-arched Roman bridge. From here one can admire the beautiful setting of the medieval town, the Haute Ville, clustered amongst narrow cobbled lanes and spring blossoms below the ruined castle of the Counts of Toulouse on the opposite bank.

The Roman Ruins
Excavations have uncovered two areas of the Roman town: the Puymin and the Villasse quarters. Both testify to the comfortable existence of the wealthier citizens, especially the vast Maison des Messius of the Puymin quarter and the elegant house of the Patrician of the Silver Bust, complete with hanging gardens and private bath, in Villasse. Also to be seen are the various mosaics, colonnaded shopping streets and (in Puymin) the museum and theatre – entered through a tunnel. The theatre's stage was carved out of the rock, allowing details such as curtain holes and pits for stage machinery to survive.

Notre Dame Cathedral
Visible against a backdrop of wooded hills from the Villasse quarter, the 12th-century cathedral, built in a mix of styles, has several points of architectural interest, particularly the barrel-vaulted cloisters. The foundations of the apse and apsidal chapel utilize columns and capitals acquired from Roman structures. The cloisters and the Roman remains can be visited on a combined ticket.

Festivals
Between July and August each year there is a summer festival, including folklore, drama and music amongst its performances, and every third year the Choralies are held, involving choral groups from around the world. Information can be obtained from the Bureau du Festival (tel 12 61 81 03; from April tel 90 36 06 25 or 90 36 24 79).

Accommodation
If possible try to stay in the quiet of the Haute Ville, in the 16th-century charm of, for example, the 3-star Le Beffroi (tel 90 36 04 71), a comfortable hotel overlooking the modern and Roman towns. Otherwise the Hôtel du Théâtre Romain (tel 90 36 05 87)

and La Piscine (tel 90 36 05 95) both offer large, clean and inexpensive rooms near the Syndicat d'Initiative in the Place du Chanoine Santel. There is also a campsite on the banks of two rivers by the Cultural Centre (tel 90 36 06 91). Alternatively, a few miles out of town near the village of Crestet the Ferme de Fontveille (tel 90 36 01 58) offers camping facilities plus a marvellous view of the Baronnies and Mont Ventoux. Dormitory beds are available too.

Restaurants
The Place de Montfort is alive with cafés and brasseries, not that there is any shortage elsewhere in the town. Michelin recommends Le Bateleur, Place Th. Aubanel, near the Roman bridge.

Nyons

Nyons is a pleasant small town of about 6300 people, lying 16 km (10 miles) north of Vaison along the D938 between the Tricastin plain and the mountains of La Lance and Veyronne. You could do much worse than make it a base for leisurely trips in the Baronnies, the Montagne de Bluye or even Mont Ventoux itself.

Sheltered by the surrounding hills, rich in exotic plants, and set in the midst of olive groves and orchards, the town has an agreeable climate all the year round and a painterly quality in the light. Its specialities include truffles, fresh and preserved fruit, lavender and Haut-Comtat wines. Although it has, in the main, attracted retired people and others who value the mildness of its winter climate, it has more than enough of interest to justify a 2-star Syndicat d'Initiative (tel 75 26 10 35) in the Place de la Libération.

In fact, the lack of world-famous monuments makes it all the easier to enjoy the quiet old district, the Quartier des Forts, and the hump-back, 15th-century bridge over the River Eygues (or Aygues, as it is still occasionally spelt). The Place du Dr Bourdongle is arcaded, as all good squares should be. There is a pleasant 8 km (5 mile) walk or drive to the north-west of the town, along what is known as the Promenade des Anglais et de Vaulx.

Accommodation and Restaurants
A restaurant conveniently situated for the Promenade des Anglais and the old quarter is Les Oliviers in Rue Escoffier which gives good set menus for reasonable prices. Central hotels include the Caravelle (tel 75 26 07 44), though it is without a restaurant, and the Colombet (tel 75 26 03 66) opposite the Syndicat d'Initiative.

Dentelles de Montmirail

Immediately south of Vaison-la-Romaine stretch the hills known as the Dentelles de Montmirail with forested conical peaks in the north rising to exposed needles of Jurassic limestone to the south. These foothills of the Ventoux range more than compensate in character for what they lack in stature – 735 m (2410 feet) is the highest peak.

The strong red Gigondas wine is produced in this region and named after one of the villages in the area. Raised to the status of an *appellation* in 1971, it has come to rival Châteauneuf-du-Pape in quality.

Séguret

A 'must' to visit is the village of Séguret, designated one of the most beautiful villages in France.

To reach it, leave Vaison by the D977 and take the D88 fork to the right after approximately 6 km (3½ miles). A further few miles bring you to a T-junction. To the left, perched on a hill, is the old village which can only be entered by foot through a covered passage. The Mascarons fountain, the clock-tower with its typical Provençal wrought-iron bell-cage and the cobbles of the narrow main street all contribute to Séguret's irresistible charm.

Below the church of St Denis in the old village is the excellent restaurant of La Table du Comtat. Though expensive, for a quiet meal watching the sun set over the Rhône Plain it couldn't be bettered. Tables should be booked in advance (tel 90 46 91 49). Rooms are also available.

The oak- and pine-covered hills behind the village make for excellent rambles – information can be obtained from the youth hostel-cum-*gîte* (tel 90 46 93 31) found on the right fork of the T-junction. The hostel also has Séguret's finest view of the Dentelles de Montmirail – across a vineyard and pastures – and is particularly attractive in the late afternoon light.

Mont Ventoux

With its rounded summit, a wasteland of white gravel that is snow-capped in winter and visible even on the haziest of days, Mont Ventoux dominates much of the Provençal landscape. Correspondingly its top offers a 360-degree panorama including all the salient features of the area and beyond: to the north, the Baronnies; to the east, the Montagne de Lure and the Lubéron; to the south, the Vaucluse Plateau and Alpilles; and to the west, the Rhône Valley and the Cévennes. However, a cloudy day or even just a midday haze can detract significantly from these magnificent views. A calm as well as a clear day is best for an ascent, as the 1909 m (6262 ft) summit is seldom free from wind and can be anything from 10°C to 20°C cooler than the lower slopes.

The Ascent
Although Mont Ventoux is accessible by car during the summer months, from November to May all or part of the road may be closed (telephone Mont Serein 90 36 03 20 for information).

Leave Vaison by the D938 and at Malaucène turn on to the D974 to reach the summit via the winter-sports resort of Mont Serein. A kilometre or so outside Malaucène a square chapel stands where there was once a pagan temple. A little further on, the road passes a shaded pool of clear green water filled by springs emerging from the foot of a cliff. This is the Source Vauclusienne, past which the road climbs through pasture and pine forest and the view gradually expands until reaching its zenith at the viewing table on the south side of the summit observatory. From here you can either return the way you came or continue to Sault, via Le Chalet-Reynard.

An attractive alternative to the above is to circle the mountain either to the north – passing through the villages of Entrechaux, Pierrelongue and Brantes before heading for Sault – or to the south via Le Paty, Ste Marie Madeleine and Le Chalet-Reynard.

North of the Ventoux Massif

The ruins of Entrechaux castle above its village form an enchanting focal point for the first stages of the northern circuit of the Ventoux. After starting from Vaison along the D938, take the D54. Then, as the Ouvèze Valley closes in, you become aware of the intriguingly sited church of Pierrelongue, high on a pinnacle of rock, making one wonder how its construction was achieved. The village is reached via the D13 then the D5.

To continue the circuit take the D72 3 km (2 miles) beyond Pierrelongue. This skirts the Montagne de Bluye as it follows the River Derbous past the straits of the Plaissans Clue, with the exposed Rocher St Julien of the Baronnies on the left. After this a series of hairpin bends lead up to the Col de Fontaube. Although a car park and viewpoint of sorts have been made here, facing back the way you have come, the views on the way up are of more interest.

Brantes
Shortly after the Col you come to the village of Brantes, with one of the most picturesque views in the whole Ventoux. Perched above the predominantly wooded Toulourenc Valley, Brantes faces the summit and piebald northern slopes of Mont Ventoux.

After Reilhanette you complete this trip via the D542/D942 to Sault, driving along the eastern flank of Mont Ventoux and the Vaucluse Plateau. From Vaison to Sault is 53 km (33 miles).

South of Mont Ventoux

The road to the south of Mont Ventoux combines the best of the two routes already described with the added advantage that the lusher vegetation and softer southern slopes of the Ventoux region are easier on the eye than the harsh and gullied northern ones. There are, too, frequent glimpses of the Dentelles de Montmirail and the Vaucluse Plateau.

As the road climbs towards Le Chalet-Reynard the typical indigenous Provençal vegetation of cypresses, broom and wild herbs gives way to stands of pine, oak, cedar and beech, with many enticing places for a picnic or walk. Not to be missed on the way is the Ste Marie Madeleine monastery. Unfortunately not open to the public, this fine example of early 11th-century Provençal Romanesque architecture can nevertheless be admired from the road.

To continue this route, leave Malaucène by the D938, taking the D19 to Bédoin after a mile or two. At Bédoin join the D974 for the winter ski-resort of Le Chalet-Reynard. Here the road joins that from the summit, giving the possibility of a 54 km (34 mile) circuit finishing back at Malaucène, or else, from either route, carry on to Sault, 20 km (13 miles) away by the D164.

Le Barroux

A little over 3 km (2 miles) further along the D938 from the D19 turnoff off is the small village of Le Barroux. From the terrace of its restored Renaissance château there is a near 360-degree panorama of the Dentelles, Vaucluse and Ventoux. The village itself is a delight, with doorways framed by the magnificent untamed roses so characteristic of the South, a vista at the end of every street and cherry orchards on its southern slopes. The shaded front terrace of the Hôtel Geraniums (tel 90 62 41 08) is a good place to relax with a drink and escape the heat of the sun, while the meals are cheap and good.

Sault

A small, sleepy town with a population of 1200, Sault lies in the heart of lavender country on a knoll above the River Croc. As you arrive from Ventoux you pass a terrace, at the northern end of the town, which commands a good view of the Vaucluse Plateau towards the Nesque Gorges. The church is worth a visit, particularly for the broken barrel-vaulting of the nave, and there is a local museum (open June to September). Of the hotels, the Deffends (tel 90 64 01 41) is the most comfortable and has a swimming-pool and gardens but is closed from October to March, inclusive. Sault's specialities are honey and nougat.

Routes South from Sault
From Sault there are two routes south. The first is to Apt, a town well placed for excursions into the Lubéron and the Vaucluse. The second is to Carpentras and so back to the Rhône Valley. This second route takes in the Nesque Gorges.

The D943 to Apt provides a fine country drive. Initially giving views over the rolling lavender fields of the Vaucluse Plateau, the road soon enters the oak and hazel woods of the Bois de Défens and the Forêt de Javon. 15 km (9 miles) from Sault, the Château Javon is a massive yet elegant 16th-century castle with a delightful but unfortunately private ornamental garden. Shortly after Javon the road descends through a picturesque gorge and the Lubéron Regional Park to St Saturnin-d'Apt – a typical hilltop village of the Vaucluse Plateau. Apt lies 9 km (6 miles) further south, making a total of 37 km (23 miles) from Sault.

The Nesque Gorges

The D942 from Sault passes along the right bank of the wild and impressive gorge of the River Nesque, whose sparsely wooded sides are enlivened by jagged limestone outcrops. The most impressive view is provided by the Belvedere viewpoint, which at 734 m (2408 ft) allows full appreciation of the gorge's depth. In the distance towers the Ventoux Massif.

From the Belvedere viewpoint the road descends through a series of short tunnels. One hairpin bend beyond the fourth tunnel there is a fine view back upstream to the Cire Rock. Deserted roadside hamlets, with houses backing onto walled-up caves, have old paths leading both up and down the now forested slopes of the gorge. Occasional terraces make ideal picnic spots. Once out of the gorge, keep to the D942 through Villes-sur-Auzon and Mazan to reach Carpentras, 45 km (28 miles) from Sault.

Carpentras

Carpentras is a lively country town with a history that adds charm rather than mere weight and possesses a skyline impressively dominated by Mont Ventoux and the Dentelles of Montmirail. It has undergone many changes over the years, many of them for the better. Once the centre of a region that was comparatively barren, the immediate countryside was transformed into an area of fruit crops and market gardens by the partial diversion of the River Durance through the Carpentras Irrigation Canal. The most celebrated local speciality is a kind of boiled sweet based on caramel called a *berlingot*. The Syndicat d'Initiative is at 170 Avenue Jean-Jaurès (tel 90 63 00 78).

The town was the capital of the Comtat Venaissin – territory belonging to the Holy See – from 1320 to the French Revolution, and might well have become the seat of the Papal Palace during the Great Schism (1378–1449), which drove the Popes temporarily from Rome, if Pope John XXII had not preferred Avignon. It was also a centre of an important Jewish community in the 16th and 17th centuries. Later, Henri Fabre, the great French entomologist, taught here for several years in the 19th century.

The Cathedral and Other Sights
Points of particular interest include the ancient Cathedral of St Siffrein, with its flamboyant Gothic and somewhat mysterious Porte Juive, or Door of the Jews, through which Jewish converts passed to be baptized. The synagogue itself is France's oldest, and is all that remains of a ghetto once occupied by 1200 Jews. There is also a Roman arch believed to be coeval with that of Orange, and the Porte d'Orange is the last remaining fragment of the town's original ramparts.

Offenbach Festival
From 15 July to 15 August, Carpentras co-hosts the Festival 'Offenbach et Son Temps' with Vaison-la-Romaine. Held in the open air, theatre performances include operettas, ballet and music.

Accommodation
One of the better hotels in Carpentras is the 3-star Safari (tel 90 63 35 35). Located on the Avignon road it offers an open air swimming-pool, tennis courts and kitchenettes for its guests. More central is the Fiacre (tel 90 63 03 15), though it has no restaurant. The Rapière du Comtat near the Porte d'Orange is cheap yet good, but the best restaurant in the area has to be the Saule Pleureur (tel 90 62 01 35) on the Avignon road (D942) 6½ km (4 miles) outside Carpentras, a little beyond Monteux.

The Vaucluse Plateau

The hilly, largely forested Plateau stretches from the Ventoux Massif in the north to the Lubéron mountains in the south and is bordered to the east and west respectively by the Albion Plateau and the D938 between Carpentras and Cavaillon. The Albion Plateau, a speleologist's heaven with its underground cave systems, is also the source of the Fontaine-de-Vaucluse, the most impressive of the area's many natural springs, closely associated historically with the Italian poet Petrarch.

Pernes-les-Fontaines

6 km (4 miles) due south of Carpentras is Pernes-les-Fontaines, which was the capital of the Comtat Venaissin from 968 to 1320 – that is, before Carpentras was. It is a typical Vaucluse township, busy with growing and preserving cherries, strawberries, melons and grapes for the market. Yet, somewhat strangely for a French town, Pernes has chosen to hide its charms, leaving its sights unsigned. Hotel accommodation is difficult to find too, though the Syndicat d'Initiative has details of rooms and apartments to let.

As you enter the town on the D938 from Carpentras, you will find the Syndicat d'Initiative on your left by a large car park. Just behind is the River Nesque which, due to concrete channelling and its small size, could easily be mistaken for an open drain. However, if you follow this upstream, a five-minute walk brings you to the main sight of the town – the old bridge. On the right-hand side the largely ruined ramparts rise up to meet the 16th-century gateway that dwarfs the bridge and tiny pavilioned chapel at its centre. Through the gate you will find a splendid 17th-century fountain, while the Clock Tower – the keep of the castle of the Counts of Toulouse – presides over the whole scene.

Routes from Pernes
For Fontaine-de-Vaucluse you should leave Pernes by the D938

Provence of the Rhône Valley

heading for L'Isle-sur-la-Sorgue but turning off on to the D25 just
before reaching it. Fontaine-de-Vaucluse is then 5 km (3 miles)
along the D25.

Fontaine-de-Vaucluse

Situated close to the cliffs that mark the western edge of the
Vaucluse Plateau and with the already broad River Sorgue running through the village, Fontaine-de-Vaucluse is attractive in its
own right. However, its popularity has, for many centuries,
derived from the *fontaine* which rises from the foot of the cliffs
half a mile away and is reached by a well-trodden track. The SI (tel
90 20 32 22) is open from Easter to October and is situated in the
Place Eglise.

On arrival by car you will be directed by a traffic policeman to one
of the car parks. Then, unless you dawdle for refreshment in the
village, it's an easy 15-minute walk along the bank of the river to
the fountain, passing beneath the ruins of a once-watchful medieval castle. There are two other places of interest on the way. The
first is the 'Underground World of Norbert Casteret' – a collection
of Casteret's speleological finds, including limestone stalagmites
and stalactites (closed from November to February). The second
is a paper mill where the entire process of paper manufacture by
traditional methods can be watched, free of charge.

The Fontaine
The famous fountain, one of the strongest resurgences of underground water in the world, is the reappearance above ground of
an important subterranean river fed by the rainfall up on the
Vaucluse Plateau and the Ventoux Massif. Most dramatic in
spring or winter when a veritable torrent of water surges away
down the boulder-strewn riverbed, the summer water-flow is a
mere trickle in comparison. But even then the tranquillity of the
site and the 400 m (1312 ft)-deep pool of turquoise water
encircled by cliffs cannot fail to affect one as forcibly as it did the
poet Petrarch. Try to time your visit towards the end of the
afternoon when the sun is on the cliffs.

It was at this spring that Petrarch met his ever-unattainable Laura,
who both bewitched him and drove him to despair. An often
quoted, but none the less delightful letter of his reads, in part: 'All
day long I wander among the bare mountains, the cool valleys
and the grottos... I have made this place my Rome, my Athens,
my homeland.'

Accommodation
1 km back along the D25 there is a splendidly situated youth
hostel (tel 90 20 31 65). Unfortunately there is little to commend
the other accommodation available in the village.

L'Isle-sur-la-Sorgue

From Fontaine-de-Vaucluse rejoin the D938 and turn left into
L'Isle-sur-la-Sorgue. This town enclosed within two arms of the
River Sorgue was originally a fishing village. Later the well-
watered site was further improved by its inhabitants through the
cutting of canals between the two arms, so that the village has
been described as the 'Venice of Vaucluse'. The Syndicat d'Initiative (tel 90 38 04 78) is in the Place Eglise.

The town's two principal sights are the church and Hôtel-Dieu, or
hospital. The church is interesting for its fine baroque interior, the
hospital for its richly decorated 17th- and 18th-century interior,
but equally for the Moustiers pottery on display in the 17th-
century pharmacy. However, it is the avenues of great plane trees
lining the canals, the waterside cafés and the charm of the little
town, enhanced by remains of Renaissance houses and slowly
revolving waterwheels, that tempts the visitor to linger.

Accommodation
A modest but friendly and attractively sited canal-side hotel is Le
Bassin (tel 90 38 03 16). More expensive, 2-star establishments
are the Araxe (tel 90 38 40 00) and Les Nevons (tel 90 20 72 00),
both with swimming-pools and gardens.

Cavaillon

Cavaillon, 10 km (6 miles) south of L'Isle-sur-la-Sorgue, again on
the D938, is as firmly associated with the fragrance of melons as
Collioure is with anchovies, but, on the whole, more agreeably,
unless you are a passionate anchovy fan. The Romans established a trading centre on the fertile plain here, close to the
confluence of the Durance and Coulon rivers, and served by the
main routes between Arles and Italy. This became the prosperous
Roman town of Cabellion. It was laid waste by barbarian
invaders, but arose again so successfully from the ashes as to
become a bishopric of some importance until the French Revolution. Now a still-expanding modern town, albeit surrounded by
acres of market gardens, there is little to detain one outside the
immediate vicinity of the Place François-Tourel – though it could
be a convenient base for excursions into the Vaucluse Plateau or

Provence of the Rhône Valley

the Petit Lubéron. The Syndicat d'Initiative is in La Rue Saunerie
(tel 90 71 32 01).

St Jacques Walk
At the junction of Place du Clos and the Place François-Tourel,
there is a small, finely decorated Roman arch which was found
more or less hidden behind the cathedral and transferred to its
present site, stone by stone, in 1880. Here also begins, to the left of
the arch, Cavaillon's most popular little outing, by footpath to the
Chapelle St Jacques. Just after the inscription to Mistral at the
second bend, ignore the steps leading up to the left unless you
are fond of rock-climbing. The path eventually comes out on to a
small plateau by a viewing table, the best views facing south from
the Lubéron round to the Alpilles and including the Durance
Valley. The restored 12th-century chapel itself lies hidden by an
enclosing wall and tall cypresses and pines. Reasonable care is
needed on the way down for the less sure-footed. The trip, there
and back, takes about three-quarters of an hour.

Other Sights
A little north of the Place François-Tourel, the 12th-century
cathedral of Notre Dame et St Véran has a fine apse and gilded
17th-century carvings framing a number of pictures. The small
18th-century synagogue contains elegant Louis XV woodwork
and a noteworthy wrought-iron balustrade around the minister's
reading desk. The Jewish Comtat Venaissin Museum in the
synagogue's basement contains a collection of historical relics.
Both are open to the public for a small admission charge. There is
also a museum of local archaeological finds and mementoes of
the old hospital in which the museum is housed. Again a modest
admission fee is charged.

Accommodation
Conveniently placed for the sights in the Place du Clos is the Hôtel
Parc (tel 90 71 57 78). Comfortable and reasonably priced, the
Parc lacks a restaurant. But if this encourages a visit to the
excellent Nicolet restaurant in Place Gambetta so much the
better. The Prévôt, 353 Ave Verdun is also to be recommended.

Gordes

One of the most picturesque of the Vaucluse's hilltop villages,
Gordes has become a fashionable summer retreat for French
artists and intellectuals from as far afield as Paris. This influx over
the last 40 years has reversed a previous decline and resulted in
the restoration of much of the village. For Gordes, leave Cavaillon

by the D2 and 15 km (9 miles) later turn off on to the D15. On the last corner before the village you are greeted by a superb view of the houses, interspersed with trees and colourful gardens, rising up in terraces over the rock promontory. To the right is the green of the Imergue Valley and in the distance Roussillon. The Syndicat d'Initiative in the Place Château (tel 90 72 02 75) is only open from April to September.

The Renaissance château, its austere frontage belying an ornate interior, houses Vasarely's Musée Didactique – a showcase of the artist's geometric paintings and sculptures. The festival of music and theatre in early August attracts internationally known performers, many giving sideshows in the village's squares. These sights aside, Gordes is an attractive place in which to relax in shaded cafés or to potter through the streets admiring the work of local artisans.

Accommodation
Hotels include the very comfortable 4-star Domaine de L'Enclos (tel 90 72 08 22) with fine views towards the Lubéron mountains plus swimming and tennis. More affordable but still comfortable, if not luxurious, are La Mayanelle (tel 90 72 00 28) and Le Provençal (tel 90 72 01 07). Most of Gordes' hotels are closed for the early part of the year until March.

Around Gordes
The nearby Village des Bories, 3 km (2 miles) south-west of Gordes and reached via a bumpy road off the D2, gives a fascinating glimpse into the rural life of the area as it was up till the 18th century. *Bories* are beehive-shaped dry-stone huts with pointed roofs only found in the southern Vaucluse and northern Lubéron. Some are of considerable antiquity and appear to have been used not only as shelters or shepherds' bothies, but also as primitive homes.

3 km (2 miles) north of Gordes lies the Abbaye de Sénanque, on a side road off the D177. It is well preserved despite being attacked by the Protestant Vaudois and sold after the Revolution. Today, owned once more by the Cistercian Order, the stunning 12th-century abbey set in an arid ravine is used for exhibitions and concerts (tel 90 72 02 05 for details). Admission is charged.

Roussillon

Remarkable for its site and in particular for the vivid contrast between the orange-red soil and the dark green of the cedars and pines, the village of Roussillon is again a fashionable retreat for painters and writers. The houses built from locally quarried ochre reveal its many shades, while the now largely abandoned quarries bear fanciful names inspired by the contorted cliff faces. The promontory to the north of the village gives a view of the Vaucluse Plateau, Mont Ventoux and, to the south, the Grand Lubéron.

The Lubéron

Running east from Cavaillon are the Lubéron mountains, one of Roman Provence's principal ranges, which rise above 1000 m (3280 ft). The chain is divided into the Petit and Grand Lubéron by the Combe de Lourmarin. As with the Vaucluse Plateau, with which the Lubéron has much in common, the area is characterized by hilltop villages built around natural strongpoints or clustered beneath castles for fear of marauding bands of Saracens. From the 13th to 16th centuries, the Vaudois, a Protestant sect violently opposed to reform, used these mountains as a stronghold from which to burn and pillage the area's churches. Eventually, during a crusade sent against them by François I in 1545, over 2000 of the sect were brutally killed. Many more fled to what is now Switzerland. The hill-farming life here was at best hard and impoverished and the devastating earthquakes at the end of the 19th century caused many villages to be abandoned in favour of the more easily cultivated plains. Only recently has this disinheritance been reversed by the arrival of artists and other summer residents who, as in the Vaucluse, have set about restoring the more picturesque villages, notably Oppède-le-Vieux and Lourmarin.

The Petit Lubéron and Tête des Buisses

Today the lush vegetation and startling variety of spring flowers of the Petit Lubéron, exemplified by the pleasant drive to the Tête des Buisses peak, give little indication of a violent past. Leave Cavaillon by the D973 towards Cheval-Blanc and then follow the signs to Vidauque. At the T-junction turn right up the hill. The road climbs steeply, giving glimpses over the market gardens of the Durance Valley towards Cavaillon and the Alpilles. From Tête des Buisses a forest road runs over the top of the Petit Lubéron – the Massif des Cèdres – to Bonnieux. However, it is not always open. After the peak, the road descends to meet the D973, and the scenery becomes more dramatic with views east down the Lubéron chain and over the top of the Régalon Gorges. To complete the 25 km (16 mile) circuit, return to Cavaillon by the D973.

Gorges du Régalon

Roughly 5 km (3 miles) further east along the D973 from the Tête des Buisses circuit is the turn-off for the Gorges du Régalon. From the car park a path leads through some scrub to an olive grove, the other side of which is the entrance to the gorge. The olive trees, poppies and bare rock make a picturesque scene. However, the path through the gorge doubles as a stream bed so that the walk should only be attempted in dry weather – a flood-marker at the entrance gives an indication of how quickly a trickle can become a torrent after rain. The path, and walk, end in a large cave at the far end of which an incredibly narrow passage – 29 m (95 ft) in height but still no more than a vertical slit in the rock – forces you to retrace your steps.

Oppède-le-Vieux

One of the most attractive hilltop villages, despite originally having been a mining centre, Oppède sits huddled within its ancient walls on the northern slopes of the Petit Lubéron 11 km (7 miles) from Cavaillon. Standing above the Coulon Valley and the Vaucluse Plateau, Oppède's best views are from its 11th/13th-century church. The village is reached via the D2, D29 and, finally, D176 roads.

Apt

Apt is a sizeable place, known as the 'capital of crystallized fruits', and is easily reached from Cavaillon by the D2 then the N100, a journey east of 31 km (19½ miles). With a permanent population of around 12,000 it is a busy commercial centre – being also the major source of ochre in France – yet preserves tree-lined walks along the bank of the Calaron, old ramparts and the first French sanctuary dedicated to Ste Anne, the mother of the Virgin. There are still pilgrimages (annually on the last Sunday in July) to the Basilica-Cathedral of Ste Anne, built in the late 11th or early 12th century, where legend has it that Ste Anne's body was brought. Aside from crystallized fruit, the town's specialities include truffles and lavender essence.

But above all Apt is a centre for fine drives into the Lubéron, the Vaucluse Plateau and to the Rustrel Colorado. The Syndicat d'Initiative (tel 90 74 03 18) in Avenue Ph.-de-Girard, can give details for excursions into the surrounding countryside and the Colorado.

The Rustrel Colorado

The Rustrel Colorado is a series of large ochre quarries 11 km (7 miles) north-east of Apt, where, as at Roussillon, excavations have left fascinatingly shaped cliffs and ridges. These are best seen from a path off the D22 road that fords the River Dôa and leads up to the viewpoint.

Around the Grand Lubéron

An easy circuit of 40 km (25 miles) south of Apt via Saignon, the Mourre Nègre and Fort-de-Buoux serves as a good introduction to the Grand Lubéron as a whole.

Saignon
Saignon is reached by the D48 from Apt and sits high over the Calaron Valley, indistinguishable at a distance from the large promontory of bare rock at its northern end. Inside the village, the charming square is surrounded by creeper-covered houses (one of which is open as an auberge some of the time) and has on its south side the old communal wash-house. The church, a little further up the hill, is worth a visit for its beautiful arcaded apse.

Saignon to the Mourre Nègre
A small unnumbered road leaves Saignon heading south-east for Castellet, a hamlet now taken over by lavender distilleries. In Castellet the road joins the D48 again, the right fork of which will take you to Auribeau. A scenic road for most of its length, the D48 gives fine views over the Vaucluse Plateau towards the Montagne de Lure and back along the Lubéron chain, including the Mourre Nègre – marked by the Paris-Nice television mast. Shortly after Auribeau a forest road climbs up to the left. If open, this can be followed to a parking area, from which the Mourre Nègre peak is a 45-minute walk.

The Mourre Nègre
The highest peak in the Lubéron range at 1125 m (3690 ft), the Mourre Nègre affords an extensive panorama, taking in the Ventoux and Lure massifs to the north, the Durance Valley and Mont Ste Victoire eastwards, right round to the Berre Lagoon in the south. To the west are the Crau Plain and the Alpilles.

Fort-de-Buoux

Once back on the D48, continue towards Saignon but turn off just outside the village on to the D232 for Bonnieux. 6 km (4 miles) later this road crosses the D113 and the right arm of the D113 will take you to Fort-de-Buoux. On the way these two roads pass through an attractive, cultivated part of the Grand Lubéron with clustered or single stone bories and occasional hamlets adding extra interest to the enchanting scenery. Near Buoux the D113 enters a picturesque gorge and the fields give way to scrub and limestone cliff-faces.

The Fort
The Fort-de-Buoux, found to the left after some houses, was for centuries a strongpoint commanding the Aigue Brun Valley. Although largely razed by Richelieu in 1660, the remains are well worth the 15-minute walk from the car park.

2 km (1 mile) beyond the fort, still on the D113, a lone tower marks the site of the ruined Prieure de St Symphorien. Then this road meets the D943, which follows the Aigue Brun River down through the gorge of Combe de Lourmarin to Lourmarin itself. Alternatively, you can turn right for Apt to complete the circuit.

Lourmarin

Lourmarin is best seen from the south across the vineyards and orchards bordering the D27. The town is capped by the rolling peaks of the Grand Lubéron to the north and overlooked to the west by its château, a ruggedly simple castle that is part 15th-century, part Renaissance. Once abandoned to the gypsies who regularly halted here on their pilgrimage to Les Stes-Maries-de-la-Mer, the château is now occupied by the Aix-en-Provence Academy and has been restored to much of its former splendour, as has the town. An admission fee is charged for entry. It is closed on Tuesdays from November to March inclusive. The Syndicat d'Initiative (tel 90 68 10 77) is in Avenue Philippe-de-Girard and is open from June to October.

Albert Camus
Lourmarin is associated with Albert Camus, the Nobel Prize-winning French novelist, who died in l960 and is buried in the village cemetery along with Philippe de Girard who invented a flax-spinning machine in the 19th century. De Girard's birthplace is now a museum which can be visited for a small charge.

Accommodation
A little outside the town, 1½ km (1 mile) along the D56, is the 3-star Hôtel du Guilles (tel 90 68 30 55) offering modern facilities plus swimming and tennis.

Cadenet

Cadenet, just under 5 km (3 miles) further south, has a locally famous statue in the main square. This is of a young drummer boy, the 'Tambour d'Arcole', and commemorates the heroism of André Etienne, born in Cadenet. During Bonaparte's fierce battle with the Austrians at the Pont d'Arcole, in Italy, in November 1796, Etienne swam across the river and beat the 'charge' signal on his drum from the other bank. The Austrians, fearing that they were under attack from both sides, retreated. Unfortunately the statue, and the town, are rather less interesting than the story. However, the church does contain a fine 3rd-century sarcophagus font.

Aix-en-Provence

From Cadenet the D943/543 continues south, crossing the Durance and the D561, until it joins the N7, where a left turn takes you to Aix-en-Provence, just under 30 km (19 miles) from Cadenet, or 54 km (34 miles) from Apt.

As befits the ancient capital of Provence, with a permanent population of 125,000 – and heaven knows how many more visiting or merely passing through the town in peak season – Aix has a 4-star Syndicat d'Initiative (tel 42 26 02 93) in the Place du Général de Gaulle. This is open all year round (though only for mornings and evenings on Sundays and holidays) and provides maps of the town with suggested walks, offers guided tours and, particularly useful during the festival period, a monthly guide to local events.

'Good King René'

Historically and culturally, Aix is one of the most interesting towns in France. So rich, indeed, is its background that any visitor spending more than a few days here might well find the pleasure of the holiday enhanced by a little digging into the corners of the past. There is, of course, the story of the Roman general Marius, whose crushing defeat of the Teutonic invaders in 102 BC is said to be the origin of the name of the Montagne St Victoire. A period of greater interest, from the point of view of the more positive arts of peace, was the reign of the monarch still known as 'Good King René'. The Counts of Provence had, since the 12th century, made the court at Aix a centre of cultural and literary refinement, a process which reached its point of highest development in the 15th century under King René. René, Duke of Anjou, titular King of Sicily and Count of Provence, was a classical scholar who was also familiar with the Hebrew and Catalan tongues. He was a skilled musician, both composer and executant, painted, wrote poetry and was a student of the sciences as well as of law. He also introduced the muscat grape into Provence and encouraged popular festivals with the object of preserving ancient folklore and the traditions of chivalry. The court over which he presided was one of the most cultivated in Europe.

Count Mirabeau
In the 18th century Aix saw the rise of Count Mirabeau, whose extraordinary career culminated in his turning his back on his peers in 1789 and getting himself elected as a representative of the Third Estate – the people.

Even today, crowded and bustling, car-parked and, at times, noisy, Aix retains much of its 18th-century elegance, with many of the sober, dignified great houses of the period still a pleasure to the eye. Splendid tree-lined avenues – the Cours Mirabeau is superb – fountains, walks, old corners and quiet squares abound. And, to add to these pleasures, there are always the delicious calissons – the almond-flavoured sweets which are as much a part of Aix as the Cours Mirabeau itself. At Palette, a couple of kilometres east of Aix, they serve a wine which goes particularly well with the local sweets and confectionery.

Thermal Baths
Aix also harks back to its Roman days, when it was called Aquae Sextiae, in providing curative waters of all kinds. And its thermal establishments offer relief from a great variety of ailments.

The Cathedral Quarter
The local sights, apart from the old town itself, include several museums and the cathedral. The Cathédrale St Sauveur combines a variety of architectural styles from the 5th to 16th centuries. The main points to be seen are: the 5th-century baptistry – a pool surrounded by eight Roman pillars with foundations believed to date back to a shrine of Apollo; the richly carved west-door panels dating from 1504; and the famous triptych of the Burning Bush – painted by Froment in 1475, and depicting (in side panels) King René and his queen in prayer, with Tarascon and Beaucaire castles in the background. To see the triptych and door panels one must ask the sacristan. Adjoining the cathedral are the delightful, Romanesque cloisters which lead to the Tapestry Museum containing the Beauvais tapestries, nine of which are taken from Natoire's Life of Don Quixote. (An entrance fee is charged.) South of the Cours Mirabeau, where King René can be seen clutching a bunch of muscat grapes, is the aristocratic Quartier Mazarin. Here is found Aix's most famous fountain, the 17th-century Four Dolphin Fountain, and the Granet

Provence of the Rhône Valley

Museum housing fine Dutch, Flemish and French paintings and an archeological room with Greek, Roman and Ligurian sculptures and Egyptian mummies.

Cézanne's Studio

Sadly, there is little to commemorate Aix's most illustrious son, Paul Cézanne, apart from his old studio that has been reconstructed as it was at his death in 1906. His easel, palette etc are displayed but only three of his paintings. The Atelier Paul Cézanne is roughly five minutes' walk from the town centre.

Music Festival

The world-famous international music festival takes place in July and early August and is an altogether much smarter affair than those of neighbouring towns (consequently it is much more expensive). However, it is preceded by a fortnight of less formal concerts, including jazz, string quartets, etc. that are generally free. Rock concerts, exhibitions and street entertainers all add to the carnival atmosphere prevalent at this time of year.

More permanent sources of entertainment are cinemas, jazz clubs and night clubs kept alive out of season by the town's 40,000 students of literature and law (the only faculties left of a great university founded in the 15th century). Not surprisingly, Aix recently polled the highest number of contented citizens of any town or city in France (Montpellier came second).

Accommodation

Aix has numerous good hotels, ranging from the 4-star Le Pigonnet (tel 42 59 02 90), Paul Cézanne (tel 42 26 34 73) and, in Celory on the N7 approach to Aix, the quiet Le Mas d'Entremont (tel 42 23 45 32), down to modest but adequate no-star establishments. Of these you might try the Hôtel Sully (tel 42 38 11 77), the Cardinal (tel 42 38 32 30) or the Hôtel Pax (tel 42 26 24 79). Restaurants also abound, but for value it is best to avoid those around the Cours Mirabeau and instead head for the Place des Cardeurs. A notable exception is the Michelin-recommended Clos de la Violette (tel 42 23 30 71) for which reservations are needed. A little way out of the town are several campsites and on the Marignane road (D9) there is an 18-hole golf course (tel 42 24 20 41) at about 9 km (5½ miles) from Aix.

Avignon

Avignon is ideally sited on the confluence of the Rhône and Durance rivers, surrounded by its still-intact ramparts and crowned by the spectacular medieval Palace of the Popes. As the main city of the Vaucluse Department it has thrived and expanded but never lost sight of its historic past, so that the old town remains the heart of the city where the Bacchanalian excesses that characterized the Popes' rule live on, revitalized by the annual festival. Petrarch, so dismayed by the iniquitous goings-on under the Popes, described Avignon as '...an abode of sorrows, the shame of mankind, a sink of vice... where God is held in contempt, money is worshipped... Everything breathes a lie: the air, the earth, the houses, and above all the bedrooms.' This may overstate contemporary activities, but the principle has not been lost.

Avignon is well served by roads and so is easily accessible from neighbouring towns. From Orange there is either the A7, the Autoroute de Soleil, or the N7; from Carpentras the D942; from L'Isle-sur-la-Sorgue the N100; from Cavaillon the D973 then the N7; and from Arles the N570. It therefore makes an excellent base from which to explore the lower reaches of the Rhône Valley, especially the towns of Tarascon and Beaucaire and, in the Alpilles, St Rémy-de-Provence and Les Baux (an equally viable base would be Arles). Nearer Avignon, Villeneuve-les-Avignon and Châteauneuf-du-Pape are well worth visiting. The Office de Tourisme is situated at 41 Cours Jean-Jaurès (tel 90 82 65 11).

Palace of the Popes
The Palais des Papes is probably the major historic attraction of Avignon. This massive example of medieval civil and military architecture was built in the 14th century for the Popes Benedict XII and Clement VI. The great walls, with their eight towers, enclose the Clementine Chapel, built over the Great Audience Chamber; two chapels with 14th-century Italian frescoes; Clement VI's chamber and the stag room, both notable for their wall paintings; and many other items of architectural and historical interest. However, those expecting something along the lines of an English stately home may be disappointed by the lack of furnishings, due to looting after the Revolution. The Palace's spell as a barracks and then prison have not helped either. A charge is made for admission. Some parts of the palace, including Benedict XII's chapel, now in use as a departmental records office, can be visited only if permission is applied for in advance. Before entering follow the walkway around the building – with each corner bringing fresh sections into view the scale of the place becomes fully apparent, as does the elegance of its unassailable walls from the garden on the east side.

Provence of the Rhône Valley

The Petit Palais Museum

At the far end of the Place du Palais, the Petit Palais houses a fine collection of early Italian art, the remnants of a collection Napoleon III had hoped to use as the nucleus for a French equivalent to the Victoria and Albert Museum. It was from this former episcopal palace that Pope Clement V, who instigated the move of the papacy from Rome, ruled. The Papal Court later became established in Avignon with the building of the Palais des Papes, begun by his successor Benedict XII.

Le Parc des Rochers des Doms

Above the Petit Palais and with superb views of the Rhône, the Pont St Bénézet and Villeneuve, these gardens, normally a pleasant place to relax from the rigours of sightseeing, catch the full force of the mistral winds – notoriously violent in Avignon – as they whistle down the Rhône Valley.

Other sights are the already mentioned Pont St Bénézet or Pont d'Avignon of nursery rhyme fame, now reduced to four arches from the original 22, and the Calvet Museum – an eclectic collection, bequeathed by a local doctor, of wrought-iron works, various antiquities (particularly Greek) and 16th- to 20th-century French paintings. The south-east quarter of the old town is well worth a visit and contains the church of St Didier, notable for its altarpiece and 14th-century frescoes, the Rue des Teinturiers and the Lapidary Museum, with exhibits from the several civilizations that have inhabited the area.

Drama Festival

The Avignon Drama Festival, founded originally by the late Jean Vilar, who created the National People's Theatre in France, is no longer confined to the art of the theatre, but now includes classic and experimental music, ballet and films. The setting, in the great courtyard of the Palais des Papes, is magnificent, but it is not easy to find seats if you have not booked well in advance. Other venues such as the municipal theatre and nearby cinemas are also used. Tickets are sold by the Syndicat d'Initiative but for information telephone 90 86 24 43 or write to Bureau de Festival, BP 92, 84006 Avignon. The Festival takes place in early July and August.

Accommodation

There is no lack of accommodation in Avignon. The 4-star hotels are the Hôtel d'Europe (tel 90 82 66 92) with its 16th-century charm, and the Hôtel Les Frênes (tel 90 31 17 93). Medium-priced establishments include the Bristol-Terminus (tel 90 82 21 21) and the Fimotel (90 82 08 08) which has a very reasonably priced restaurant. Unpretentious but adequate accommodation is provided by the Hôtel le Parc (tel 90 82 71 55) and the Hôtel Central (tel 90 86 07 81). Don't forget though that in the peak holiday period (July and August) Avignon, which already has a permanent population of 90,000 odd, attracts enormous numbers of tourists, so that you are likely to find even the city's ample hotel resources under heavy strain and the streets crowded. However there is an organization – CEMEA – that arranges short stays during the festival period as well as seminars. Reservations may be made through CEMEA, 76 Boulevard de la Villette, 75940 Paris (tel 42 06 38 10) or during the festival at Rue Frédéric Mistral (tel 90 86 50 00). The Ile de la Barthelasse, on the Rhône to the north of the town, has several campsites.

Restaurants

Avignon has a quite bewildering range of restaurants, from the excellent Hiely (tel 90 86 17 07 for reservations) in the Rue Republique and the Brunel at 46 Rue Balance to many modest establishments offering set menus for under 60F. Amongst these are the city's many Vietnamese restaurants. A good place to start is the Rue des Teinturiers, an old cobbled street alongside the Sorgue and once the haunt of dyers, which has quite a few small restaurants and cafés. The Place de L'Horloge, named after the clock-tower whose two figures – the Jacks – still chime the hours, has many cafés enlivened by buskers and other street artists.

Villeneuve-les-Avignon

Originally a French frontier town facing the Holy Roman Empire (i.e. Avignon) across the Rhône, Villeneuve was fortified by successive kings. The 14th-century Fort St André is one of the finest examples of military architecture of its period. Both the fort and the Philippe-le-Bel tower – the fortification of the Villeneuve end of the Pont St Bénézet – have excellent views of Avignon, Mont Ventoux and the Alpilles. Later, as overcrowding in Avignon forced cardinals across the river, Villeneuve enjoyed long-lasting prosperity curtailed only by the Revolution. This is reflected now in the strange juxtaposition of past splendours and present decay that typifies this rather sleepy town of under 10,000 souls. The SI (tel 90 25 61 33) is found in the Place Ch-David.

The town's principle sights, after the fortifications, are two works of art – a further result of the Popes across the water was the development of a sophisticated cultural centre that attracted the likes of Petrarch and Simone Martini, the Siennese painter. The two works – an exquisitely carved ivory statue of the Virgin from the 14th century, and a magnificent 15th-century altarpiece by Quarton depicting the Coronation of the Virgin – are found in the sacristy of St Marc's church and the Municipal Museum, respectively. They can be visited on a combined ticket (both places are closed on Tuesdays and for the whole of February).

The altarpiece, like many of the museum's exhibits, originated in the Chartreuse du Val-de-Bénédiction. Once inhabited by monks of the Carthusian Order, whose cells can be seen leading off the cloisters, the charterhouse is now used for exhibitions and other cultural events. Details of the summer programme can be obtained by ringing 90 25 05 46. Also originating in the charterhouse is the Pietà now hung in the Louvre in Paris. Depicting the Virgin and others mourning over the dead body of Christ, the Pietà, also attributed to Quarton, is considered by some to be the first true French masterpiece.

Accommodation
Aside from art, Villeneuve and the adjoining Les Angles are interesting to stay in with their old corners and fine views. Indeed, from some of the terraces, the sight of a storm gathering in the Rhône Valley, and the first breath of wind, are truly dramatic. Places to stay include Le Prieure (tel 90 25 18 20) which, offering swimming, tennis and an excellent restaurant, is hard to better. A slightly more modest alternative is La Magnaneraie (tel 90 25 11 11).

Châteauneuf-du-Pape

Châteauneuf-du-Pape lies roughly midway between Avignon and Orange, to the west of the N7. From Avignon leave the N7 just after Sorgue for the D17 which leads to Châteauneuf itself. If approaching from Orange the simplest route is to take the D68, a minor road, all the way, though however you decide to do it the route is well signposted. Distances are 18 km (11 miles) from Avignon, 13 km (8 miles) from Orange.

A solitary wall and tower are all that remain of the former summer palace of the Popes who in the 14th century planted the first vineyard in what is now the heart of the Rhône wine-growing area. The *appellation contrôlée* standard was initiated here in 1923 to protect France's strongest red wine – 12.5 percent alcohol minimum – by specifiying the 13 grape varieties that can be blended by the various producers to give the classic dark and deep wine typical of a Châteauneuf-du-Pape label. The Musée des Vieux Outils de Vignerons in the Père Anselme cave gives a potted history of winemaking over the centuries along with lessons on winetasting technique. You can then go and try it out at the various caves that admit visitors free. The Syndicat d'Initiative (tel 90 83 71 08) will provide a list (closed November).

Accommodation
For somewhere to stay there is the 3-star Hôtel Le Logis d'Arnavel (tel 90 83 73 22) or, at the other end of the range, the Hôtel Mère Germaine (tel 90 83 70 72) next to the SI. Restaurants tend to be expensive and with delusions of grandeur. However, the Hostellerie Château des Fines Roches (tel 90 83 70 23) found 3 km (2 miles) south of Châteauneuf by the D17, is excellent – though book in advance.

Tarascon
Within easy reach of Avignon, 23 km (14 miles) by the N570, are Tarascon and Beaucaire, on the left and right banks of the Rhône respectively. Visitors to Tarascon will find the SI in the Rue des Halles within the old town walls (tel 90 91 03 52).

The Tarasque
Tarascon has been associated for 2000 years with a legendary amphibious monster, the Tarasque, whose habit of feeding on the inhabitants of the Rhône Valley was checked only when Ste Marthe (who had accompanied Les Saintes Maries to Provence from Palestine) sprinkled holy water on it so that it became docile and allowed the local people to cut it into pieces. The annual fête celebrating this event was initiated by King René and, recently revived, takes place on the last Sunday of July. During the revelry a huge moving model of the monster, powered by men inside, is wheeled through the streets. Tarascon will also be familiar to students of French literature from the novels and short stories of Alphonse Daudet, and in particular his comic hero Tartarin of Tarascon. Indeed Tartarin has become as much a part of the lore of Tarascon as the Tarasque itself.

The Château
But Tarascon has other rewarding aspects, apart from legends and 19th-century French literature. The great 12th-century château on the Rhône is undoubtedly one of the finest feudal castles in France and its terraces offer views that should not be missed. Completed in the 15th century by King René, the castle is in two parts – the lofty seigneurial apartments, once the King's residence, and below them the courtyard, flanked by square towers. Guided tours are conducted at set times, according to the

season, and the admission charge is halved on Sundays and holidays (closed on Tuesdays). Besides the castle is the church of Ste Marthe, a lovely 12th-century building containing the supposed sarcophagus of the saint in its crypt.

Accommodation
The best of the central hotels is the De Provence (tel 90 91 06 43) in Bvd Victor Hugo and there is also a youth hostel (tel 90 91 04 08).

Beaucaire

The château of Beaucaire faces that of Tarascon from the other side of the Rhône, though it is now little more than a shell – it was demolished on Richelieu's orders in 1632. The walls of the keep still give fine views, however. The enormous international fair, which made Beaucaire famous throughout Europe from the 13th century until comparatively recently with the advent of railways, has left little trace except in so far as the town is still a busy and lively river-port for wine. This character is enhanced by the fact that the canal from the Rhône to Sète runs along the south side of the town, flanked by the tree-lined Quai du Général de Gaulle and the Cours Gambetta.

The Syndicat d'Initiative (tel 66 59 26 57) in the Hôtel de Ville has an impressive list of houses and other public buildings worth seeing in the town and its surroundings. Hotels include the Vignes Blanches (tel 66 59 13 12) and, by the canal, Les Doctrinaires (tel 66 59 41 32).

The Alpilles

Isolated from the rest of the Lubéron range by the Durance River, the Alpilles rise dramatically from the surrounding plains in a manner belying their actual height – the highest peak, La Caume, is a mere 399 m (1310 ft). Between crests the limestone has been eroded into weird and wonderful shapes best seen in the Val d'Enfer near Les Baux – itself perched on a bluff reminiscent of the Meteora monasteries of northern Greece. The view of the Alpilles from the ancient Gallo-Roman settlement of Glanum St Rémy is one of the best in the Rhône Valley. A circuit of 24½ km (15 miles), starting at St Rémy and taking in La Caume and the historic town of Les Baux, is described below. Basically, this is a not too arduous day's drive. It would be less expensive to stay in St Rémy than Les Baux.

St Rémy-de-Provence

St Rémy is best approached by the D99 from Cavaillon 19 km (12 miles) away to the east. The poplar-lined road is capped by deceptively high peaks giving the impression of a great range but slowly resolving into the exquisite miniature of the Alpilles. On the way there are fine views of the Durance Valley from the church, Notre Dame de Beauregard, above Orgon, and the picturesque old village of Eygalières, reached via the D74A 9 km (6 miles) out of Cavaillon, makes a pleasant coffee stop. Avignon is 21 km (13 miles) away by the D571. The Syndicat d'Initiative (tel 90 92 05 22) is in the Place Jean-Jaurès.

Nostradamus and Van Gogh

A township of about 8500 inhabitants, St Rémy is one of the richest treasure-stores of Roman remains in Provence. Originally founded as the settlement of Glanon by the Greeks of Marseilles in the 2nd century BC, the ancient town was taken by Caesar in the year 49, rebuilt and renamed Glanum. Laid waste by barbarian invaders, it revived to become the scene of a legendary miracle performed by the Bishop of Reims in the year 500, or thereabouts, which gave St Rémy its present name. A house on the Avenue Hoche is reputed to have been the birthplace of Nostradamus, the 16th-century astrologer, whose predictions are claimed to have included the assassination of President Kennedy. More recently the town was connected with Van Gogh – it was in the nearby St Paul-de-Mausole monastery that he spent the last year of his life (1889–90) after cutting off his ear. The belfry of the monastery rises above the trees just north of Les Antiques and the very attractive 12th-century cloisters are worth visiting.

Les Antiques

The plateau of Les Antiques, as the Roman remains are known, is 1 km (¾ mile) south of St Rémy, and is crossed by the D5. The Mausoleum built to commemorate Caius and Lucius, Augustus's two grandsons named as his heirs who both died tragically young, and the Municipal arch are the most important Roman relics. However, for the serious student of archaeology, the site of Glanum, across the D5, with its fragments of walls and columned roadways, is of great interest. Work on the site, which began in 1921, is understood to have brought to light so far no more than a tenth of the town, which is believed to have had up to 5000 inhabitants. A detailed guide is available from the Syndicat d'Initiative in St Rémy. Finds from Glanum, such as the sculptures of Octavia and Julia found in the temples, are now housed in Hôtel de Sade in St Rémy town centre.

Accommodation
The town's leading hotels are the Château des Alpilles (tel 90 92 03 33) and the Hostellerie du Vallon-de-Valrugues (tel 90 92 04 40). Neither have a restaurant but both offer tennis and swimming. These two are closely followed by the Hôtel des Antiques (tel 90 92 03 02) and Le Castelet (tel 90 92 07 21). There are also many more modest places such as the Hôtel de Provence (tel 90 92 06 27). Most hotels are closed from mid-November to mid-March. There is a campsite just outside the town in the Chemin de Monplaisir (tel 90 92 22 70).

St Rémy to Les Baux
Go west out of St Rémy-de-Provence and along the tree-lined Avenue Fauconnet as far as the hospital, where you take the left fork on to the D37 for about 3 km (2 miles) to where it is crossed by the D27. This mountain road and then the D27A, again a left turn, will take you to Les Baux. Roughly a kilometre before the D27A, a single-track road runs off to the left. If you follow this you will arrive at a viewing table from which there is a superb vista of Les Baux and the Val d'Enfer. Further afield one can make out the Camargue, Arles, the Lubéron, and to the north-east, Mont Ventoux.

Les Baux

There is much to be said about Les Baux, but nothing the tourist is told about it can equal the first impact of this amazing citadel itself, part the work of prehistoric man, part due to the kind of rock sculpture carried out by geological and meteorological forces that can also be seen at work in the 'natural ruins' of sites like Montpellier-le-Vieux. The more out of season, of course, the greater the impact, but even in season the crowds and souvenir shops cannot diminish the strangeness and power of the site.

An Astonishing History
A mere recital of Les Baux's historic associations reads like a lunatic film scenario put forward by a Hollywood mogul during the early years of the industry. Cave-dwellers and Courts of Love; noble families with titles like Orange, Grimaldi and Les Baux; medieval splendour, squalor and brutality; powerful princesses as well as cruel lords; links with Italy and Spain and one of the Magi, King Balthasar – all these and the torchlit Christmas shepherds' mass which still goes on would have to be taken into account.

To get the full flavour of Les Baux it should ideally be visited by moonlight and out of season, although the torchlit procession in which a newborn lamb is led by shepherds to the altar in a cart drawn by a ram is a beautiful spectacle that nothing can spoil. This is not, however, the exclusive prerogative of Les Baux, being common to many of the villages of the Rhône delta and the stony stretch called the Crau. Likewise, the 16-point star which the Lords of Les Baux incorporated into their armorial devices is popularly associated with King Balthasar – to whom they vainly traced their lineage – but is also the emblem of the Camargue gypsies, who brought it from the East.

As with Tarascon, Les Baux's heyday came to an abrupt end in 1632 with the dismantling of the castle by Richelieu and the fining of the citizenry for being Protestant. On a more prosaic level, bauxite (aluminium ore), was first discovered here in 1822 and named after the village.

Today the village can conveniently be divided into three parts. Of the village proper there are the living and dead sectors, while below them, in the Vallon de la Fontaine, lie farms and a few hotels. The valley also has the Pavillon de la Reine Jeanne, King René's second wife, a charming small Renaissance building which so enchanted the poet Mistral that he had a copy made for his tomb.

The Living Village
From the car park the living village is entered by the Magi Gate. Once inside stay, initially, on the lower streets as you make your way to the Place St Vincent at the far end. On the way, small squares give views over the precipice to the valley and the old gate, Porte Eyguières, can be seen. Place St Vincent has the fine 16th-century Porcelets house (now a museum), a small chapel and St Vincent's church in which the processional lamb's cart is kept. Above the square the steep, narrow streets are lined with boutiques and houses in a mixture of styles, their unifying feature being the warm honey-coloured stone of which they are built. There are also several ancient communal baking ovens for the village's bread and a fascinating narrow lane, the Rue du Trencat, which has been hollowed out of the rock and further carved into odd shapes by the wind and the rain.

The Dead Village
The entrance to the dead village is through the small museum that exhibits finds from around the area. There is little to see in the way of buildings, but this is easily compensated for by the marvellous views of the Alpilles, especially to the east as they

stretch away in an arc enclosing a patchwork of olive groves and cultivated fields in which the red soil is exposed. To the south and west over the roofs of the living village, the Crau Plain, the Camargue and (on a clear day) the sea can be seen. Dominating the promontory is the ruined castle. It was from its keep that the Viscount Raymond de Turenne made his victims, kidnapped exclusively for this sport, leap to their deaths while he watched.

The Cathedral d'Images

About a third of a mile (500 m) outside Les Baux, again on the D27, is the Cathedral d'Images. A former bauxite quarry, the huge caverns have ingeniously been converted into a theatre for audio-visual displays with ever-changing slides being projected on to the multitude of walls, ceilings and even floors, to the accompaniment of surreal, Pink Floyd-like music.

Accommodation

In the Vallon de la Fontaine is one of the most celebrated hotels (and restaurants) in France, the Oustau de Baumanière (tel 90 54 33 07), where Queen Elizabeth II stayed during a holiday. There is also the Hostellerie de la Reine Jeanne (tel 90 97 32 06) in the village of Baux itself, while in the valley are several more establishments including La Ribolo de Taven (tel 90 97 34 23) and La Cabro d'Or (tel 90 54 33 21), both with excellent restaurants, the latter offering swimming and tennis as well. Less expensive ones are Le Mas d'Aigret (tel 90 97 33 54) and Le Mas de la Fontaine (tel 90 97 34 13). There is a golf course a little south of the village towards Maussane.

To continue the circuit, leave Les Baux heading east on the D27A, and at the T-junction where this meets the D5 turn left uphill towards St Rémy. After 3 km (2 miles) a minor road to the right runs to La Caume.

La Caume

La Caume, like most French peaks, is marked by a television relay mast. However, this one is distinguished by also having a recently erected hut used as a birds-of-prey observation point. Inside, wall charts (in French only) depict the various species found, the most unusual of which is the Eqyptian vulture, which can often be seen riding the thermals above La Caume's cliffs. The views from here embrace the Alpilles, the Crau Plain, the Camargue to the south, the Durance Valley to the east, and Mont Ventoux, roughly north. From the last shoulder on the road up to the summit there is a fine view north past the limestone crags to the plains around St Rémy. The spring flowering can be quite spectacular – beyond the observation point some of the local flora has been labelled. The area is ideal for walks; for the more adventurous the GR6 traverses most of the length of the Alpilles. A shorter walk using a section of the GR6 takes you from the mountain road downhill towards St Rémy. On the way, part of the ancient Roman canal taking water to Glanum can be seen and, after a narrow passage walled in by rock, the Mausoleum is discernible amongst the trees and eventually Glanum itself. The walk starts about 2 km (1½ miles) after the turn-off from the D5 to La Caume and is marked by a sign to St Clerg. It should take roughly 45 minutes each way.

Once back on the D5 after visiting La Caume, the circuit can be completed by heading for St Rémy 4 km (2½ miles) away. Alternatively, you can head for Arles by way of Fontveille and the Abbaye de Montmajour. For this route take the D5 to Maussane and then the D17 to Fontveille, a journey of 14 km (9 miles).

Fontveille

A pleasant town of 3500, Fontveille owes its place on the tourist map to Alphonse Daudet and his letters inspired by the windmill found a kilometre south of the town through an avenue of pines that borders the D33. Certainly the setting on the edge of a pine forest with views of the Alpilles is enchanting even if the windmill is just a windmill. There is a small museum dedicated to the author in the basement. An admission fee is charged.

Several kilometres further along the D33 and then left on the D78F, a pair of Gallo-Roman aqueducts run either side of the road. The more interesting remains are to be found south of the road and in particular the mill which represents a rare instance of the engineering of this era. The other aqueduct once supplied water to Arles.

Accommodation
Of Fontveille's hotels, the 3-star La Regalido (tel 90 97 60 22) is the best, with attractive gardens and a superb restaurant. However, it is closed from December to mid-January. La Peiriero (tel 90 97 76 10), also 3-star, and the 2-star Valmajour (tel 90 97 62 33) both offer comfortable modern facilities plus swimming-pools. For good food Le Patio restaurant (tel 90 97 73 10) should be your first choice.

Abbaye de Montmajour

4½ km (3 miles) from Fontveille by the D17, the abbey stands on a wooded knoll dominating the surrounding plains, its austere rectangular towers almost devoid of embellishment forming an instantly recognizable landmark. The abbey's history is in sharp contrast to its architecture. Founded by Benedictine monks in the 10th century, it was sacked by their 17th-century counterparts before they themselves left, due to declining prosperity. It was then rebuilt in the 18th century only for history to repeat itself, this time at the hands of antique-dealers following the disgrace of its cardinal. Thus the abbey was once more left a ruin. It is now partially restored. Points to note are the 12th-century chapel, with a crypt built into the rock, and the cloisters. A little way back down the D17 there is also the appealing Ste Croix chapel, again 12th-century. An admission charge is made for entry into the abbey. It is closed on Tuesdays.

Arles

6 km (4 miles) south of Montmajour, and 19 km (12 miles) by the N570 from Tarascon, is Arles, one of the capital cities of Roman France. Gateway to the Camargue, Arles is also a noted city of the arts, being closely associated with literature through Frédéric Mistral and Alphonse Daudet, music through Gounod and Bizet, and painting through Van Gogh. It is this last connection of which the city is especially proud – no postcard stand is complete without details of Van Gogh's paintings, although some complain of the commercialization of the artist by daubing walls with the pun 'Vin$ent'. The Syndicat d'Initiative (tel 90 96 29 35) is just off the Boulevard des Lices on the Esplanade Charles de Gaulle.

The town has grown up astride a narrow stretch of the main arm of the Rhône, the Grand Rhône, which widens appreciably south of Arles and flows in broad splendour to the Mediterranean just beyond Port St Louis. The other arm of the river, the Petit Rhône, branches off westwards just north of the town and then winds its way south to the Mediterranean near Les Stes Maries-de-la-Mer, forming the western boundary of the Camargue. But the situation of Arles was not always like this. The area we call the Bouches-du-Rhône was once a vast estuary with a few rocky islands, of which the island of Arles was one. In time the estuary became more and more silted up with the natural material brought down by the Rhône, creating the complex of marshland, sandbanks, lagoons, islets and saltmarshes we know today.

Roman Arles

Even more interesting than the changes in the physical setting of the town were the later changes in its status in occupied Gaul, when, from being a dependency of Marseilles, Arles supplanted it as the chief port. When Marseilles took sides with Pompey against Caesar, Caesar ordered Arles to build him a fleet strong enough to bring the colonists of Marseilles to heel. The fleet, according to some accounts, was delivered to him within a month. Arles was rewarded with the spoils of Marseilles and became the great sea- and river-port of the Gauls, growing century by century until the Emperor Constantine took up imperial residence here, and his successors made it the capital city of the Gauls.

Roman Arles consisted of a fortified town on the left bank of the Rhône, entirely enclosed by a wall with four gates flanked by towers, and a residential district of substantial villas on the right bank. The two halves of the town were linked by a bridge of boats. In its Roman heyday it must have been one of the wonder cities of the world, with an amphitheatre that could hold the entire population of the town, a 16,000-seat theatre, a circus, a basilica, triumphal arches here and there to remind the populace of Roman power, and baths as big as those of Caracalla in Rome. As a fair amount of this splendour has survived, there is a great deal for the visitor to see. Later Arles' importance continued as a centre of Christianity. St Augustine was consecrated the first Archbishop of Canterbury here in the cathedral of St Trophime in 597. But by the 9th century the decline had started and gradually commercial superiority was lost to Marseilles and political power to Aix, leaving Arles a backwater until the post-war advent of cultivation in the Camargue and tourism.

Ideally you might begin your visit by arming yourself with a good street plan in which the principal sights are marked and, starting from the Boulevard des Lices (site of the ancient 'lists' or tiltyard where tournaments were held), see as many of the important sites as possible, making note of those that attract you most so that, if you have time, you can return to them with fuller information from the Syndicat d'Initiative. In this way you can eliminate all those objects in which you cannot really become interested except with a positive effort of will – or a sense of duty, which has no place on a holiday trip. If this sounds extravagant in admission fees relax – an all-inclusive ticket to the eight principal sights costs around 30F compared to 10F or more each if done individually. The ticket includes the amphitheatre, the theatre, Constantine's baths, the cloisters of St Trophime, the Alyscamps

Provence of the Rhône Valley

– an ancient burial ground many times painted by Van Gogh – and the Arlaten, Reattu, Pagan Art and Christian Art museums.

The Amphitheatre

One of the earliest and largest amphitheatres of the Roman world, the Arles arena could hold over 25,000 spectators and, as in the past, is still the scene of bloody entertainment in the form of bullfights. Two kinds of bullfight are performed throughout the Camargue: Provençal ones, after which the bull is released; and Spanish-style ones to the death. Built by the architect T. Crispius Reburrus in the 1st century AD, the arena owes its survival to being converted into a fortified town of 200 houses during the Middle Ages. It was then that the three towers were added.

The Théâtre Antique

Again built during the Augustan period in the 1st century AD, the theatre is in a lamentable state due to pillaging and the removal of masonry during the Dark Ages. Of the stage wall only two marble columns survive and, in front, 20 rows of seats where once some 7000 existed. However, the site can still captivate and is now part of a walled garden with the superlative Romanesque bell-tower of St Trophime rising up above the cypresses behind the stage. Today the theatre is used for drama and dance spectacles during the summer months. Adjoining the theatre – but a long walk away – is the Jardin d'Eté, an attractive, shaded park containing a memorial to Van Gogh.

St Trophime

A former cathedral, St Trophime dates from Charlemagne's time, though it underwent extensive remodelling in the 11th and 12th centuries and again in the 15th. The resultant mix is surprisingly harmonious and the west portal is an exquisite piece of Provençal Romanesque stonework. The cloisters, too, are noted for their rich carvings depicting biblical scenes, and are considered by some to be the most beautiful in Provence. The north side, 12th-century Romanesque, is the finest of the four.

Constantine's Baths

The baths are all that remain of Constantine's Palace. Built in the 4th century and only partially uncovered they are none the less impressive in size.

The Museum of Arles

The Arlaten Museum – or Muséon Arlaten, to give it its Provençal title – was created in 1897 by the ever-present poet Frédéric Mistral, who also contributed towards its maintenance the entire sum of the Nobel Prize which was awarded to him in l904. The collection, which is displayed in a 16th-century private mansion – l'Hôtel de Castellan-Laval – gives a comprehensive survey of the costume, arts, crafts, popular art, trades, music and folklore of the region. The staff wear traditional costume and many of the exhibits are labelled in Mistral's own hand.

Picasso and Rousseau
The Reattu Museum, in the former 15th-century priory of the Knights of Malta, is named after the painter who once owned the building. Aside from his works there are collections of Rousseau watercolours, of contemporary photographic works and, above all, a permanent collection of 57 drawings donated by Picasso to this town he so adored.

The impressive Museum of Pagan Art consists of Greek and Roman tombs, such as the white-marble sarcophagus of Hippolytus and Phaedra, mosaics and statues found locally and two casts of the Venus of Arles dug up in the theatre – the original is in the Louvre. The Museum of Christian Art also has sarcophagi – from the Alyscamps – but its principal attraction is the underground gallery, or cryptoporticus. This served as a granary during imperial times and helped to feed Rome's population.

The Alyscamps Necropolis
Dating from Roman times, and later consecrated by the Christians, the Alyscamps was once one of the most famous and prestigious necropolises in Europe and completely encircled the city. However, since the Rennaissance the site has gradually been denuded of its finer sarcophagi, leaving only those arranged along the length of the avenue up to the church of St Honoratus. It was this avenue and church that inspired Van Gogh's several paintings of the Alyscamps – or Elysian Fields. The avenue is a jumble of trees particularly attractive in the spring when the blossom is out. The church is a fine example of early Provençal Romanesque notable for its rare octagonal belfry.

Festivals
Arles hosts a number of festivals each year, the most notable of which are the Rencontres Internationales de la Photographie and the dance and music festival held principally in the Théâtre Antique and the Alyscamps. The photographic festival consists of two weeks of exhibitions, slideshows and workshops, details of which can be obtained from the Syndicat d'Initiative. Information on the drama and music festival is dispensed by ADCA, La Mairie, Place de la Republique, 13200 Arles (or tel 90 93 98 10). Both take

place in July. On 1 May each year the Fête des Gardiens, a rodeo of sorts, takes place in the arena after a parade through the town. There is also bull-running in the streets and the town is well equipped with cinemas, theatres and music venues.

Other Attractions
The market constitutes a good-natured mayhem that encompasses most of the town centre each Saturday morning. Although prices might not differ much from those of a supermarket, the sheer variety of goods for sale makes the market an essential part of a visit to Arles. Anything from grandfather clocks to goat kids can be bought here as well as some of the best fruit and cheeses to be found.

Arles generally has an extensive range of Provençal food and wines, with local emphasis on dishes prepared with Camargue rice and the celebrated smoked sausage of Arles. Best of all, since this is the south, sit in the sun (or the shade) in the Boulevard des Lices, the public gardens, by the Rhône, in the Place de la Republique, or in a café under the trees, and read about the places you will visit when the sun goes in.

Accommodation
Arles is well supplied with hotels, ranging from the 4-star Jules César (tel 90 93 43 20) in the Boulevard des Lices and the 3-star D'Arlatan (tel 90 93 56 66) near the old Roman forum – both of which occupy period buildings – to the 1-star Hôtel de Provence (tel 90 96 03 29) and the Petit Hôtel de L'Arlésienne (tel 90 96 11 36), with marvellous views of the arena from its rooms. The youth hostel (tel 90 96 18 25) is found in the Avenue M. Foch, by the municipal sports centre and stadium. There is also a choice of several campsites on the route to St Martin-de-Crau, 17½ km (11 miles) east by the N453. The nearest is Camping City (tel 90 93 08 86) just outside Arles, with two more in Raphèle-les-Arles, 12 km (7½ miles) away. The Syndicat d'Initiative gives out a booklet with a comprehensive list of accommodation in the area.

Restaurants
The list of restaurants is even more extensive than that of the hotels. Generally speaking, there are two main areas for cafés and restaurants – the Boulevard des Lices and the Forum. The former is slightly more expensive but has the advantage of being an excellent place from which to watch the Saturday market. However, there are several other equally pleasant but smaller squares in which to enjoy a meal or a drink. Lou Gardian (tel 90 96 76 15) serves generous, good meals at excellent value and is popular

with tourists. One of the best restaurants is the Lou Marques, a part of the Hôtel Jules César.

St Giles

16 km (10 miles) due west of Arles by the D572 lies St Giles. Once the gateway to the Camargue, St Giles is now known chiefly for the west front of its abbey, though it remains a lively and friendly small town. The abbey has suffered over the centuries during times of unrest such as the Albigensian Crusade, the Wars of Religion and the Revolution, so that all that now remains of the original 12th-century structure is the west front itself. However, the three doorways are richly carved, depicting the life of Jesus with statues of the Apostles in the embrasures, and are well worth a visit. Inside the abbey, the crypt contains the tomb of St Giles which, in times past, was one of the four great Christian pilgrimage centres. An admission fee is charged for the crypt.

The Syndicat d'Initiative (tel 66 87 33 75) is in the Maison Romane just above the abbey. Hotels include Le Cours (tel 66 87 31 93) and Le Globe (tel 66 87 30 41), both with good-value restaurants.

The Camargue

The Camargue is an area of 56,000 hectares (roughly 140,000 acres) of alluvial deposit and salt-marshes between the two arms of the Rhone, extending from just north of Arles, where the river divides, to the sea. Between the vast Etang de Vaccarès (about 15,000 acres) at its heart, and the sea, is what can only be described as a watery desert of salt-marshes, dunes, *étangs* (land-locked pools), lagoons and salines.

The Saline Bird Sanctuaries

The salines, enclosed by long sweeping sandbanks and a maze of dikes, constitute an area 'twixt wind and water which only the expert can safely negotiate but are worth a look even if only from the roadside. Owned by the Salin du Midi corporation, the salines are used for sea-salt production – huge, shimmering piles of which can be seen waiting for refining – but double as the favoured haunt of flamingos. This is especially true of the salines near Salin-de-Giraud in which exists the only breeding colony of flamingos in Europe. During the summer months this can be seen from the Digue-la-Mer dike, which runs through the salines, as a huge mass of birds. There are approximately 10,000 breeding pairs in the Etang du Fangassier with countless others either feeding by sieving the water for its minute animal fauna or simply resting on one leg in the adjacent salines.

Many other fascinating birds are to be found throughout the Camargue – bee-eaters flit along the canals, egrets ride the backs of bull and horse alike, and marsh harriers fly low over the reeds. Purple herons, numerous waders and waterfowl are also to be found along with others, depending on the time of year.

As one of the largest staging-posts in bird migrations between Northern Europe and Africa, the Camargue has been a Mecca for ornithologists for decades and the site of much important research. Thus while serious birdwatchers are welcomed, casual visitors and photographers are generally discouraged, at least within the reserves.

Much of the traditional Camargue remains; plants such as sali-cornia and tamarisk that thrive on salt feed the herds of wild bulls which still roam the area, while in the Rièges islands, south of the Etang de Vaccarès, spring sees a marvellous display of wild flowers. Yellow flag irises abound along the canals during the month of May. However, this facet of the Camargue is restricted to the various reserves that combine to protect a significant proportion of the area but are consequently difficult to gain access into. The National Reserve of the Etang de Vaccarès is open only to bona fide naturalists and other scientific workers, who must apply well in advance to the Conservateur de la Reserve, M. J. de Caffarelli, 2 Rue Honoré-Nicolas, Arles, for permission to visit the area. However, for the casual visitor there is an information centre on the east side of the Etang at La Capellière which gives a good feel for the area and its wildlife. Here, too, the more recent arrivals in the Camarge can be observed. The coypu, once the scourge of the East Anglian waterways, is found in large numbers on the canals of the Camargue and is most easily seen towards dusk. In appearance like a small beaver, its burrows do not cause the same damage as in England as the water-level here is below that of the ground. Beavers themselves still inhabit the area but are extremely rarely sighted, their presence being only apparent through the occasio-nal gnawed tree.

The Gardiens
The bulls bred for beef or, from Spanish stock, for the bull-running and cockade-snatching sports of Provence, are herded by *gardiens*, with their cowboy hats and trident goads. They also guard and round up the tough locally bred horses which are said

to be of a very ancient breed. Of the horses only the stallions are traditionally ridden, the white mares being allowed to roam semi-wild with the cattle.

Outside the reserves, the Camargue, waterlogged and salt-impregnated, is, nevertheless, anything but a sterile wasteland or a vast romantic solitude, but the cultivation of its resources has demanded an unremitting struggle. Drainage, desalination and irrigation with fresh water go on continuously, and throughout the northern part of the Camargue, grapes, rice and other cereals are cultivated. Indeed, the abundant water supply combined with the climate have enabled the rice crop (originally grown to prepare the land for other crops) to exceed in yield per acre the production of tropical rice countries. And this is despite the efforts of the flamingos, which during a nocturnal feeding session can decimate a paddy field (hence the continual background 'shotgun' noise of birdscarers).

Unfortunately parts of the Camargue, like the life of the gypsies, have been grossly commercialized and vulgarized to meet what is (predominantly erroneously) believed to be the universal tourist taste. But there is still much of interest, beauty and strangeness, and for those who are drawn to areas where land and water are intermingled almost indistinguishably, there is still a magic that no other kind of landscape can convey.

Visiting the Camargue
There are three principal ways of visiting the Camargue: one for those dependent upon public transport; one for the motorist with the time and the interest to look further; and one (already mentioned) for the specialist.

A reconnaissance trip by tourist bus from, say, Montpellier or Arles is by no means the worst way of getting a glimpse of the Camargue as the commentary is usually well informed and helpful. For details and bookings visit the relevant Syndicat d'Initiative. But better is to hire a bicycle and explore from one of the holiday centres such as Les Stes Maries-de-la-Mer. Bicycles also have the advantage of allowing you on trails closed to motor vehicles. A trail map can be obtained from the SI in Les Stes Maries, as can details of horse-rides and rentals. Don't be put off by the sight of pseudo-Wild West ranch-houses with hitching posts, there is good riding if you have a reliable guide.

Alternatively, there are a number of routes from Arles which will give you a better idea of the Camargue as a whole. You can take

Provence of the Rhône Valley

the D570 via Albaron to Les Stes Maries-de-la-Mer, a trip of 40 km (25 miles) that includes some of the best of the accessible Camargue around Pioch Badet, though also the worst on the approach to Les Stes Maries. 4 km (2½ miles) outside Les Stes Maries is the Parc Ornithologique but unless you find the spectacle of wild birds (including flamingos) mooning around in restricted places to be totally irresistible, a visit to the Parc is not recommended. Much better to watch the marshes yourself for free-roaming bulls or egrets. To this end, on the return journey from Les Stes Maries, leave by the D85A past the Mas Cacharel to Pioch Badet. The road is bordered on both sides by marshes and the typical stunted vegetation of the region.

A more extensive look at the area would be to again start on the D570 from Arles but to turn off after about 3 km (2 miles) and follow the D36 to Salin-de-Giraud. This road follows the Grand Rhône almost to the sea, though the river is hidden behind a screen of trees. The scale of the cultivation of the Camargue can be seen as field after field appears, separated from its neighbours by a windbreak of cypresses or reeds. Le Sambuc, a one horse-town where the landscape begins to open out more and resemble the 'traditional' Camargue, boasts one of the best restaurants in Le Trident. There is also a very good homemade pizza van on Sundays. The D36 continues past Salin-de-Giraud and, as the D36D, ends at the Plage de Piemanson having skirted the eastern edge of the salines. The beach, 48 km (30 miles) from Arles is a broad sweep of sand hard enough to be driven on. However, during the summer a secluded spot is hard to find. There is also considerable local feeling against those who come in convoys of four-wheel-drive vehicles and proceed to tear up the dunes that back on to the beach, as evinced by the slogan '4 × 4 GO HOME' found all over the Camargue.

Salin-de-Giraud itself has little to offer, though you have to pass through it to reach the Digue-la-Mer. Once the other side drive through Faraman before taking the dirt track that eventually becomes the dyke passing between the Fangassier and Galabert salines. For most if not all of its length the track is pot-holed and in generally poor condition but should be passable even after rain. Side tracks lead to beaches and the shanty town of Beauduc near Le Phare lighthouse. Throughout the summer a caravan is positioned by the Fangassier pool. Here two naturalists both guard the flamingos and dispense information on them.

After the Digue head north along the D36B. Roughly 11 km (7 miles) after you rejoin the tarmac, you will pass a marsh on the right-hand side of the road marked by one of the traditional white, inverted-boat-shaped huts of the *gardien*. The marsh, a part of the Tour du Vallat Foundation, is both a much-used flamingo feeding-site and a beautiful example of the Camargue as it once was. A short distance further on the road borders the Etang de Vaccarès, giving a couple of good viewpoints over the lagoon and passing the Reserve Information Centre at La Capellière. At Villeneuve turn left on to the D37 towards Albaron. Again the road skirts the Etang de Vaccarès for much of its length before meeting the D570 to Les Stes Maries, 39 km (24 miles) from Villeneuve.

Les Stes Maries-de-la-Mer

Les Stes Maries-de-la-Mer is best known as a place of pilgrimage for the gypsies who are especially devoted to Sara, the black servant who, according to tradition, accompanied the two St Marys — Mary Jacoby, sister of the Virgin, and Mary Salome, mother of the Apostle James the Greater and John, when the boat in which they had drifted from Palestine ran ashore. Having founded a simple place of worship dedicated to the Virgin on this spot, the disciples separated (also in the frail craft were the resuscitated Lazarus and his sisters Martha and Mary Magdalen, as well as Maximin and Sidonie). Martha went to preach the gospel in Tarascon, Mary Magdalen continued her penitence at St Baume, Lazarus went to preach at Marseilles, Maximin and Sidonie went to Aix. The other two Marys and Sara stayed in the Camargue where a rapidly growing cult developed round their remains, which were buried in a simple oratory they had founded. The SI (tel 90 47 82 55) is in the Avenue Van Gogh.

The Church
The church that replaced the original oratory was fortified in the 9th century against the Saracens and incorporated in the ramparts of the town. This was replaced by the present, still-fortified structure in the 12th century which now dominates the white-washed houses of the town and the marshes for miles around. The church contains the enshrined relics of the saints and also the statue of Sara, the patron saint of the gypsies, that form the centrepieces of the two pilgrimages and religious ceremonies that take place each year — on 24 and 25 May and the nearest weekend to 22 October. During the celebrations the shrines and statue are carried through the town to the sea accompanied by traditionally dressed Arlesians, *gardiens* and gypsies. Days of secular festivities then follow with horse-racing, bull-running and dancing. Every three or four years, it is believed, the gypsies use this occasion to elect a new queen.

Provence of the Rhône Valley

However, this aspect of Les Stes Maries is gradually being overwhelmed by its dual role as a tourist seaside resort. In fact often the only gypsies to be seen are those begging by grabbing and reading palms. Yet the town is still attractive with many lively boutiques and enticing restaurants despite inflated prices. The town's beaches are probably the best to be found in the Camargue, particularly those along the coastal trail to the east of the town. On the other side there is a marina, the bullring and, typical of the South, a carousel.

Accommodation
There are numerous hotels to be chosen from, including many places between Les Stes Maries and Pioch Badet which have adapted the traditional hut of the *gardien* into comfortable rooms, such as the 4-star Le Pont des Bannes (tel 90 47 81 09) on the Arles road. In the town itself are the Des Amphores (tel 90 47 80 31), the Mas Sainte-Hélène (tel 90 47 81 15) and the less expensive Méditerranée (tel 90 97 82 09). There is also a youth hostel at Pioch Badet (tel 90 97 91 72) and two campsites, one to the east of Les Stes Maries by the sea, the other on the banks of the Petit Rhône (tel 90 47 84 67 and 90 97 85 99, respectively).

Aigues-Mortes

Aigues-Mortes is reached by the D570 then the D58 from Arles, 47 km (29 miles) to the north-east. From Les Stes Maries-de-la-Mer it is 33 km (21 miles) following the same road numbers. Alternatively, leave Les Stes Maries by the D38. 6 km (4 miles) out of town a ferry will take you across the Petit Rhône from where the D85 and the D58 lead to Aigues-Mortes through the Petite Camargue.

Of the Camargue's towns, Aigues-Mortes is arguably by far the most interesting and attractive. Its amazingly well-preserved and sun-baked walls – a complete enceinte of 13th-century ramparts with its magnificent Tour de Constance – enclose a small town which has, in spring at least, all the charm of a southern village. It is a holiday resort with a lively centre of shops, restaurants, narrow streets full of character, and little squares, but entirely without the plastic tattiness of small towns on sea-fronts. Aigues-Mortes ('Dead Waters') is in fact about 6 km (4 miles) from the sea, amid marshes, lagoons and salt-flats. It is both historic, being founded by Louis IX (St Louis) as a base for his crusade – in 1248 – to the Holy Lands, and alive; its charm lies as much in its extraordinary completeness today as in the past, and in its uniqueness among walled towns. The Syndicat d'Initiative (tel 66 51 95 00) is in the Place St Louis, the town's central square (closed from mid-October to mid-November).

The Old Town Walls

From the Tour de Constance you can walk the ramparts in about three-quarters of an hour – an experience not to be missed, even if a fee is charged. The ramparts include 20 towers of various shapes and sizes and ten gates or narrow entries; the total effect is that of a community which, having found a good life, was determined to defend it, rather than the usual medieval impression of a stronghold from which its builder spent all his time looking for someone to attack. Not that the towers are totally without a bloody past. One, the Tour des Bourguigons, was named after the Burgundians who, in 1418, during the Hundred Years War, were massacred by the attacking Armagnacs and whose bodies were piled inside the tower and salted to keep until burial. The Tour de Constance was for five centuries a political prison – courageous yet pathetic graffiti inscribed on the walls by Huguenots can still be seen.

Accommodation and Restaurants

Although Aigues-Mortes is probably more of a place to visit for the day rather than to stay in, there are several reasonable hotels such as the Hostellerie des Remparts (tel 66 53 82 77) and the nearby Hôtel le Victoria (tel 66 53 64 55). The town within the walls has several good restaurants with a local flavour, such as the Camargue in the Rue Republique. However, as with the hotels, the cheaper ones are found outside the walls. Of these, make for the Hôtel l'Escale (tel 66 53 71 14) which offers good-sized meals at very reasonable prices. Prominent on the menus of many restaurants such as this on the fringes of the Camargue is the local dish of *boeuf gardien* – a simple beef stew on a bed of rice.

Le Grau-du-Roi and Port Camargue

From Aigues-Mortes the D989 runs south-west for 6 km (4 miles) between the Midi salines and the Grande Roubine – the canal that feeds the salines with Mediterranean sea-water. Both the canal and the road end in Le Grau-du-Roi, originally a fishing village, but now a resort centred around the two café-lined streets that border the canal. With better beaches, and somehow more attractive despite consisting entirely of modern buildings, is Port Camargue, a kilometre or two to the south. A purpose-built resort,

Provence of the Rhône Valley

Port Camargue's low-rise, modular hotels and villas are built on promontories projecting into the port, creating a vast marina with a mooring for everyone. The pleasure craft, gardens and flower-filled balconies make an attractive whole.

Le Grau-du-Roi's Syndicat d'Initiative (tel 66 51 67 70) is in the Boulevard Front-de-Mer; Port Camargue's (tel 66 51 71 68) is closed from October to March inclusive. The 3-star Hôtel le Spinaker (tel 66 51 54 93) in Port Camargue has a good restaurant.

St Etienne-de-Tinée

Alpine Provence

There are two main routes south from Grenoble to the Côte d'Azur between Marseilles and St Raphael. The N75, with various detours, gives the first full promise of the South once you are over the Col de la Croix-Haute and continues through Sisteron, Peyruis, Forcalquier, Manosque and Brignoles to Toulon. The N85, which forks left from the N75 about 10 km (6 miles) south of Grenoble at Le Pont-de-Claix, goes through Gap, Sisteron, Digne, St André-les-Alpes, Castellane, Draguignan, Le Muy, Fréjus and St Raphael. There is also a hair-raising third (summer) route along the N202 via Barcelonette and St André-les-Alpes.

South through Sisteron

Sisteron is reached by way of Aspres-sur-Buech (altitude 762 m/ 2499 ft) and Serres. Aspres is a mountain village with a natural mineral spring, caves, picturesque ruins, a 2-star hotel, Le Parc (tel 92 58 60 01), and a campsite. Serres (680 m/2230 ft), is a most attractive little town built on the slopes of a rocky promontory overlooking the River Buech, a site which has been fortified since the 10th century. Its riches include the splendid old Hôtel de Lesdiguières, a 12th-century church, a chapel cut out of solid rock, some interesting houses of the 14th, 15th and 16th centuries, and the remains of ramparts. There are three hotels, one 4-star campsite and another more modest one.

Sisteron

About 30 km (19 miles) further south and about 200 m (560 ft) nearer sea-level is Sisteron, a town of approximately 7000 inhabitants, whose population grows to 10,000 and more in the season. Driving in from the north on the N75 you cross the Buech River, which joins the Durance at the north-west corner of the town.

The indispensable Syndicat d'Initiative (2-star) is in Les Arcades, and offers an excellent street-plan, leaflets and other illustrated material. Sisteron, in its rocky setting, occupies a key position at a point where Provence and the old Dauphine meet, and has always been a strongpoint. The impressive citadel, on the summit of a rocky escarpment, still dominates the town and there is a conducted tour with sound effects. A maze of old vaulted streets leads to the Romanesque cathedral of Notre Dame, and can be conveniently explored by following the wall signs provided by the SI. In July and August there is a Festival of Music and Drama, held in the Citadel and in the Cloister of St Dominique. The surrounding country is well worth exploring, with excursions to the impressive Rocher de la Baume – the great rock that faces the citadel across the Durance – and to many attractive villages and mountain roads. Trout and game, lamb and *pieds-paquets* (sheep's tripe stuffed with garlic, onions, parsley and pickled pork), nougat, fruit and honey are local specialities.

Accommodation
There are about a dozen hotels, ranging from the 3-star Grand Hôtel du Cours (tel 92 61 04 51) to a number of modest but adequate places with only a few rooms. Some of these do not serve meals. A letter to the SI will bring the latest information, but please don't forget to send an international postal coupon for the reply.

From Sisteron continue south to Château-Arnoux, and on leaving the town turn left along the N96 through Peyruis. Between 4 and 5 km (3 miles) beyond Peyruis turn right and follow the D12 to Forcalquier (about 5 km).

Forcalquier

Forcalquier is a pleasant summer resort with four hotels –
including the 2-star Grand (tel 92 75 00 35) – a number of letting
agencies for holiday accommodation, and a useful Syndicat
d'Initiative. It has a fair range of entertainment and sport available
in the season, and a wide range of excursions is offered. It is an
excellent centre for *charcuterie* and game, as well as mushrooms
and truffles and several varieties of goat's cheese. The 12th-
century church and medieval houses ensure those quiet sun-
baked or shaded corners in which to spend a lazy southern
afternoon.

From Forcalquier drive west along the N100 for about 12 km (8
miles), or a little more, until you reach the N207, which turns off to
the left. Follow this road to Manosque, at the eastern end of the
Lubéron Massif.

Manosque

Manosque is one of those small southern towns which seem to
have had too much history and now lie basking in the sun,
content to leave the stage to others. It maintains this relaxed air,
strangely enough, in spite of being an important agricultural and
trade centre. Enclosed in its fine tree-lined boulevards, which
have replaced the ancient ramparts, it offers, in a stroll from the
ancient Soubeyran Gate to the Saunerie Gate, the epitome of a
picturesque Provençal town, with its narrow ways and tall
houses.

With 10 hotels – headed by the 3-star Hôtel les Quintrands (tel 92
72 08 86) – and an excellent Syndicat d'Initiative in the Place Dr
P.Joubert, Manosque is a good centre for exploring the valley of
the Durance, for fishing, and for many other sports. It has two
industrial zones outside the town, a flying club and opportunities
for good riding. From Manosque a leisurely drive south to the sea
at Cassis is recommended; the Syndicat d'Initiative will advise
you about the best minor roads, according to the time of year.
(Cassis is the first Mediterranean port-cum-holiday resort east of
Marseilles.)

South through Gap and Digne

Another route south in this part of the country – the N85 from
Grenoble – runs through Gap, Digne, Castellane and Draguignan
to the Mediterranean. Gap, like Sisteron, is on the Route Napo-

leon, an impressive work of road improvement which was inaugurated in l932. It marks the route followed by the Emperor on his return from Elba, when he landed at Golfe-Juan and marched to Grenoble. The Syndicats d'Initiative at all stages of the route have adopted eagles in flight as the symbol of the new road project, echoing Napoleon's phrase: 'The Eagle will fly from bell-tower to bell-tower until he reaches the towers of Notre Dame...'

Gap

Gap is mainly a place on the way to somewhere else, though the fact that its population increases in the high season from about 28,000 to 40,000 suggests that it also makes an excellent holiday base.

Indeed, there is now a 3-star Syndicat d'Initiative with ample information and advice about such places of interest in the area as the Lac de Serre-Ponçon, the valleys of the Champsaur, Devoluy, Valgaudemar and Queyras, and many lovely drives over mountain passes (Gap itself stands at 735 m/2410 ft). There are about 30 hotels in and around the town (though this includes some very small ones as well as the 3-star La Grille (tel 92 53 84 84)), a fair amount of other accommodation and excellent campsites.

Until the end of the 17th century, Gap still retained traces of its long history as a fortress town (Vapincum), but in 1692 a great fire destroyed almost 800 of its 953 dwellings. It is still, however, capital of the Hautes-Alpes Department and an important commercial centre, and has an impressive Romanesque-Gothic cathedral. The winter-sports resorts of Superdevoluy, Ceuse, Orcières-Merlette and Ancelle are within easy reach.

Continuing south, follow the Route Napoleon (N85) in the reverse direction to Napoleon, through Sisteron to Château-Arnoux, then stay on the N85 to Digne.

Digne

Digne-les-Bains (to give it its full title) is one of the best-known stopping places for travellers between Grenoble and the Côte d'Azur, but it is well worth a more leisurely stay. Capital of the Alpes-de-Haute-Provence Department (not to be confused with the Hautes-Alpes Department, of which Gap is the chief town), it stands on the left bank of the River Bléone and has many attractions, not only as a health resort with a well-known thermal establishment, but also as both a summer and a winter resort. The original settlement was at the foot of Mont St Vincent, where the village was huddled round the church of Notre-Dame du Bourg, but the present town grew in a more defensible position on the slopes of Mont St Charles. The church is all that now remains of the earlier centre.

The cathedral of St Jerome, heart of the 'new' town, was built at the end of the 15th century, partly on the site of the old fortified château which defended the settlement. The medicinal hot springs are a couple of kilometres away to the south along the D20, on the right bank of the Torrent des Eaux Chaudes, which joins the Bléone at Digne. Unusual among French towns, Digne has named its main thoroughfare the Boulevard Gassendi, to commemorate not a politician or a general but a philosopher (1592–1655) who became Professor of Philosophy at Aix when he was only 25, and had many important discussions with Descartes. Digne is well placed for a day-trip to the gorges of the Verdon and many other beauty-spots. There are about 15 reasonably priced hotels and pensions (including three in the 3-star category) and the Syndicat d'Initiative rates three stars.

Castellane

South-eastwards from Digne the N85 goes to Castellane and on through Grasse to the Riviera east of St Raphael. From Castellane you can turn on to the N555 which leads to Draguignan. Castellane is a health resort on the Verdon River, surrounded by mountains, woodland and fields ranging up to 1980 m (6494 ft). It is also probably the most practical base for a visit to the Grand Canyon of the Verdon, which makes an unforgettable whole-day trip from the town. Castellane itself, which stands at 724 m (2375 ft), has considerable charm with its fine central square, the Place Marcel Sauvaire, a Romanesque church, pentagonal tower, Clock Gate, old ramparts and Napoleon bridge, as well as the Chapel of Notre-Dame du Roc, outside the township, from which there are fine views.

There are nine comparatively small family hotels and a large number of mainly high-grade camping and caravan sites in the neighbourhood, details of which can be obtained from the Syndicat d'Initiative, Castellane.

From Castellane the N85 (Route Napoléon) runs directly to Grasse and Cannes.

Alpine Provence

Gorges of the Verdon

The Verdon's Grand Canyon is probably unrivalled in Europe. The Verdon, a tributary of the Durance, has carved a number of dramatic gorges in the limestone plateaux of Haute-Provence, but none of them as deep, precipitous and wild as the Grand Canyon. The north side is best visited by way of the N552 west of Castellane; the south side from Draguignan or Aups. Alternatively the north side can be visited from Moustiers-Ste Marie, driving east along the N552 towards Castellane.

The south side has the breathtaking Corniche Sublime (D71), a road cut through the rock between Comps and Auguine, from which the finest views of the canyon can be seen. The gorges vary in depth from 250 m (820 ft) to 700 m (2296 ft): in width they range, at the bottom, from 6 m (20 ft) to 100 m (328 ft) and, at the top of the great cliffs, from 200 m (656 ft) to 1500 m (4920 ft). The north side has other means of approaching the canyon, and it is also possible to explore it on foot (an eight-hour project), but for this you need the right advice, preparation and clothing.

Draguignan

Draguignan, about 45 km (28 miles) south of Castellane on the N555, is the capital of the Var Department. It is a busy, lively town, best known to holidaymakers today as the gateway to the Verdon Gorges and the Maures mountains. It is one of the richest repositories of legend and folklore of the South, and there is little doubt that in the same way that Tarascon is named after a particular legendary monster, Draguignan is named after a beast so awe-inspiring as to have been known as *the* dragon, giving rise to a collection of tales that have become inextricably interwoven with the Christian tradition.

The dragon (Gaelic *drak*) which terrorized the countryside was overcome, according to tradition, by St Hermentaire, first Bishop of Antibes. Unfortunately, as most experts in this field admit, it has been impossible to find any details of the saint's achievement, though the victor is said to have built a chapel on the site, dedicated to St Michael. The hermitage of St Hermentaire can be seen when you leave Draguignan in a north-westerly direction.

One authority, quoted by the contemporary French writer Jean-Paul Clébert, suggests that the strength of the tradition, combined with the absence of details, indicates that the Dragon of Draguignan belongs to that class of infernal creatures which inhabit, and are perhaps bred, in marshes, feeding on the devil's plant, the nenuphar, nymphea or, as we call it less ominously, water-lily. Certainly these horrific products of the human imagination suggest the creatures conjured up by miasmic mephitic vapours. The fact remains that the nearby meadows of Nartuby were once part of the marshland that surrounded Draguignan.

Accommodation
Eight hotels are listed by the SI in Ave Lazare Carnot, headed by the 3-star Col de l'Ange (tel 94 68 23 01).

From Draguignan it is an easy run to the sea at Ste Maxime, Fréjus or St Raphael.

South via Barcelonnette and St André

If you are a first-class mountain driver, a third route (weather permitting) takes you south along the N202 over the Isoard Pass (2360 m/7740 ft) to Guillestre and then over the Vars Pass (2011 m/ 6596 ft) to Barcelonnette. From Grenoble to Barcelonnette by the two passes is 135 km (84 miles).

Barcelonnette

Barcelonnette, which stands at 1135 m (3722 ft) and has 3400 inhabitants, is perfectly situated as a summer and winter resort (it is practically surrounded by winter-sports centres). From Barcelonnette towards the coast every route has its scenic attractions. The N208, for example, leads over the Allos Pass (2250 m/7380 ft) through Allos and Colmar. About 9 km (6 miles) south of Colmar the road divides, the N208 continuing to Annot and the N55 bearing right to St André-les-Alpes. Taking the right fork is recommended, even if it lengthens your journey a little, for the pleasure of seeing St André-les-Alpes, a good example of the kind of mountain village – or very small town – that brings many holidaymakers back to the South year after year, and compensates in good measure for some of the more regrettable developments along the coast itself.

St André-les-Alpes

St André-les-Alpes, with its Syndicat d'Initiative in the Rue Basse, does in fact see its modest population of just over 1000 doubled in July and August, but much of the increase is absorbed by the excellent campsites in the surrounding countryside, and the village in the high season is characterized by greater animation rather than congestion. It has nine hotels, with eight in the starred categories headed by the 2-star Le Clair Logis on the Route de Digne (tel 92 89 04 05) and Le Colombier on Route d'Allos La Mure (tel 92 89 07 11). The SI also has a list of available lettings for the summer. St André loses nothing by being a little overlooked in the general publicity for this area: the visitor does not expect anything sensational and is agreeably surprised. You could do worse than take a very relaxed spell in St André and its mountain setting.

Entrevaux and Annot

From St André the N207 comes down the mountains by way of Entrevaux and Peget-Theniers to Nice, or by the N85 through Castellane and Grasse to Cannes. One of the advantages of the first route is that it takes you through Entrevaux, a lovely and still unspoiled mountain township with an ancient cathedral, a fortress, defenceworks by Vauban and a particularly fine situation. Local accommodation is limited – the only hotel being the Hôtel Vauban in the Place Moreau (tel 93 05 42 40). However, the popular township of Annot, also based on an old fortified village on the N208 about 10 km (6 miles) away, has six hotels, headed by the 2-star Hôtel de l'Avenue in Ave de la Gare (tel 92 83 22 07), and is more adequately, though not excessively, geared to holidaymakers.

Annot can also be reached directly from Barcelonnette by keeping to the N208, but this would mean bypassing St André-les-Alpes, which would be a pity.

The route through St André-les-Alpes also provides for the alternative way to the coast, through Grasse. From St André drive south along the N207 (which goes to Entrevaux and eventually Nice) until you come to a secondary road turning off to the right (N555). This takes you to Castellane, on the N85.

(For further details of alpine Provence see also excursions into the hinterland of Nice in the chapter on the Côte d'Azur.)

St Tropez harbour

Coastal Provence

The Mediterranean coast from Marseilles to Menton and its immediate hinterland – a region which falls naturally into two parts, Provence-Côte d'Azur from the Bouches-du-Rhône to St Raphael, and the Riviera-Côte d'Azur from St Raphael to the Italian frontier – has never been an entirely unalloyed paradise. Even the wealthy pioneers who first nosed it out as a winter retreat had to endure all the hardships of 18th- and 19th-century travel to get there, as well as the vagaries of an unfamiliar way of life, unfamiliar insects and food, and the strange moods and language of the local inhabitants. Even with the coming of the roads and the railways there were still mosquitoes and engine-smoke to contend with up to a quarter of a century ago, and many of us grew up with an image of the Côte d'Azur in which dazzling seas, sunlit mountains, brilliantly flower-decked little railway stations and heart-aching glimpses of lemons, mimosa or olives had to triumph over bouts of choking steam as the great trains clattered through mountain tunnels on their journey along the coast. The tideless blue Mediterranean has always been polluted to varying degrees by human waste, and some of the most charming of the older hillside residences so much admired today were the forerunners of the building blight which appears likely to leave no acre of land unspoilt.

The shores of the Lion Gulf, which stretch from Marseilles west and south almost to the Pyrenees, are still sandy but no longer inhospitable, with a string of modern, mosquito-free resorts and some of the best-equipped pleasure ports in Europe – perhaps in the world. The Côte d'Azur is still, in spite of everything, an incomparable stretch of rocky coastline deeply indented with marvellous bays, a region of natural beauty which only a geological or nuclear cataclysm could totally destroy.

At the nodal point stands Marseilles, dividing the *yin* of Languedoc and Roussillon from the *yang* of Provence, the Côte d'Azur and the Riviera. Marseilles, where, it has been suggested with justice, Gaul began and Africa begins.

Marseilles

Marseilles is the second largest city and the first port of France, with over one million inhabitants. It also claims to be the most ancient city of France, since its original founders were Ionian Greeks in the 6th century BC, and indeed one of its sailors, Pytheas, is reputed to have been the first to discover the British Isles in the 4th century BC. For many of its visitors, whatever the purpose of their visit, it has always been one of the most dramatic cities of the world; dramatic in its structure, its history, its mixture of threats and promises, its pullulating life and, at times, its enduring mystery. The ideal ways of arriving in Marseilles are still by sea or by rail. By sea for obvious reasons, and by rail because no one who ever arrived for the first time in Marseilles at St Charles Station and walked out on to the terrace that looks across the stone valley of the great city to the Vieux Port, and beyond it to the impressive, lofty mass of Notre-Dame de la Garde, is ever likely to forget it.

Like all great ports, Marseilles is rich in tall stories and ancient legends, from gross comments on the pollution content of the Vieux Port to innumerable theories – academic, folkloric, mythological or simply Gallic – about the name of the district known as 'La Belle de Mai'. The name of the main thoroughfare – the Canebière (or 'Can o' beer' as British sailors call it) – is itself said to derive from *chenevière*, meaning hemp plantation. But whereas one explanation is that in the Middle Ages the marshland round the Vieux Port was planted with hemp which was made into rope locally for rigging, another is that the word '*chenevière*' could just as well refer to a place where hemp was sold, which would naturally be near where the ropemakers worked. Wherever the truth lies, the fact undoubtedly remains that hemp – in some form or other – has always been associated with Marseilles.

Cannabis, of course, is also a form of hemp, and drug-trafficking – particularly of opium-based products such as heroin – has also given the city considerable notoriety in recent years, as exemplified in William Friedkin's 1972 film, *The French Connection*, set in Marseilles. Madame de Sevigné's description of the place as being 'a trifle roguish' thus still holds true today.

Stendhal found Marseilles the prettiest town in France in 1838 but times have certainly changed since then. Now a major contender with Barcelona and Genoa as the predominant city of the Mediterranean, Marseilles 'Europort of the South' has the second largest airport in France, is the headquarters of the Ricard Pastis empire and produces 20 percent of the world's civilian helicopters, amongst other things. However, even if it is no longer the city of Marcel Pagnol and the Vieux Port is not what it was, there is still enough of historic, social, civic and artistic interest to satisfy the most demanding traveller.

Sightseeing
For those with little time and less stamina, an easy way to orient oneself is to take a coach tour of the city from outside the Office du Tourisme (tel 91 54 91 11) at 4 La Canebière (the harbour end). Buses depart daily at 10.00, June-September except on Sundays and public holidays. Another alternative is to catch 'Le Petit Train de la Bonne Mère' – a little road train that runs around the Vieux Port area all year through (adults 25F, children under 13 15F, journey time 50 min). It departs and returns to Quai des Belges (Quai du Port corner).

Otherwise, pick up a street plan (which also contains a map of the smart modern Métro), the *Marseilles News* 'what's on' guide for the season and head off to your preferred sights. The three best views of Marseilles are undoubtedly to be had from Pharo Park overlooking the harbour – a pleasant garden surrounding the former palace of the Empress Eugenie, wife of Napoleon III – the basilica of Notre-Dame de la Garde perched high over the city,

Coastal Provence

and from the sun-bleached island prison of Château D'If situated
a short boat-ride away from the Vieux Port.

The Vieux Port
From Pharo Park you can watch the enormous Mediterranean
cruise ships docking in the modern port whilst the little yachts
flutter past into the harbour the ancient triremes once used.
Indeed a sense of history persists in the Vieux Port as an authentic
full-scale pirate galleon, the *Neptune*, is currently moored on the
Quai du Port. Built for Roman Polanski's film *Pirates* in 1984/5 it is
now open to the public and houses a film museum run by
Carthago Films.

The Old Port now largely accommodates only pleasure craft and
the surrounding quays and narrow streets are continually alive
with strollers, shops and charming little fish restaurants where
you will find the traditional dish of Marseilles, *bouillabaisse*,
prepared and eaten with great dedication to the art (indeed, there
is even a 'Guild of the Bouillabaisse Marseillaise' with 13 members in Marseilles and one in Paris). The two sturdy forts guarding
the harbour entrance are St Jean to the north and St Nicholas
(built by Vauban) to the south. And on the south side of the Old
Port near to Fort St Nicholas is the fortified Basilica of St Victor
built in the 11th century but still housing the original 5th-century
shrine constructed by St Cassian.

Château D'If
To get to the Château D'If take one of the regular hourly ferries
operating from the Quai des Belges (ferries also run to the Ile de
Frioul and the *calanques* or fjords down the coast, but prices for
the trips to the latter tend to be cheaper and more competitive
from Cassis). The trip only takes 10 min or so (32F return fare – no
cheques accepted), though you are advised to catch an early boat
in the high season as they tend to get very crowded later in the
day. Once on the island you can take your time and catch
whichever boat back suits you. There are toilets and a snack-bar
amongst the fortifications. Entrance to the château itself, where
Dumas' fictional Count of Monte Cristo and the very real Man in
the Iron Mask were incarcerated, is an extra 15F and a guide
(French-speaking only) will point out the hole through which the
Count is supposed to have escaped. (Colour brochures in English
and other languages are available.)

Notre-Dame de la Garde
For the stout-limbed, the steep climb to the 19th-century basilica
of Notre-Dame de la Garde is well worth the effort (for the rest,

the tourist coach, the little road train and a No. 60 bus also go there). The views, particularly at the end of the day when there are fewer people and the sun from the west lights up the whole city facing the harbour, are spectacular. The church was heavily sieged during the Revolution and to commemorate further action around it in the Second World War a Sherman tank has been sited a little in front of the basilica in the Place Colonel Edon. As you wander back down the slopes in search of a long, cool *citron pressé* tarry awhile to look at the statue of the city's great architect/painter/sculptor Pierre Puget 'the French Bernini', who among painters Stendhal felt came 'immediately after Poussin and Le Sueur' and whose work is widespread in Provence. (Though the graffiti on the plinth in the Jardin Pierre Puget seem to suggest that he is less than universally admired today.)

Museums
Marseilles has always been associated with the sea and the Roman Docks Museum will give you an excellent idea of the development of the town as a port from ancient times. The Maritime Museum deals with seafaring history from the 17th century to the present.

The Museum of Old Marseilles is housed in the 16th-century Maison Diamantée (notable for its unusual studded walls) behind the Quai du Port, and, for those with a car, the Borely Château just to the south of the city is worth a visit. The Egyptian and the Mediterranean Archeology sections, however, have recently been relocated in the new Centre de la Vieille Charité exhibition complex based around the Hospice de la Vieille Charité, with its Puget chapel, behind the Quai du Port. The Musée Cantini in the Rue Grignan has modern art, the Musée Grobet Labadie in the Bvd Longchamp has sculpture, tapestries and designs (14th–18th centuries), the Galérie des Transports has the history of transport and the Musée de Château Gombert has arts and traditions of rural Marseilles.

La Cité Radieuse
A good way to see some of the city's further-flung treasures is to take the Métro. From the huge 19th-century La Major cathedral built beside the remains of the original 12th-century Romanesque church take the underground from Joliette (flat fare 6.50F) in clean air-conditioned orange and yellow carriages to Rond Point du Pharo and walk along the Boulevard Michelet for about 15 min to Le Corbusier's municipal housing block (still occupied by 2000 people) known as La Cité Radieuse. For those disappointed that it seems no different than the brutalist architecture around it, a

Coastal Provence

breath of antique air may be had immediately opposite. For here, sadly not open to the public, is a picture-book mansion with beautifully tended gardens which currently houses the Conservatoire of Music. The sound of virtuoso pianists plying their trade beside the bleak expressway is refreshing indeed. (Buses 21 and 22 also go to Cité Le Corbusier.)

The Palais Longchamp

Returning on the Métro alight at Cinq Avenue-Longchamp, turn right and follow the wall of the zoological gardens around until you reach the splendid entrance to the Palais Longchamp which houses the Natural History Museum and Museum of Fine Arts (open daily 10.00–17.00, admission 6F). Don't miss the dramatically lit giant sculptures by Puget in the Salles de Puget and, if you are a fan, the three cabinets of small bronze busts by Marseilles' other famous son, the caricaturist Honoré Daumier. (Also, if you've yet to see *pétanques* or *boules* there always seems to be a game underway in the playing area behind the left wing of the Palais, beneath the gaze of yet another Puget bust.)

Shopping

Holiday shoppers will find plenty to occupy them on La Canebière (which incidentally has both a Barclays and a NatWest bank at the harbour end) and adjoining streets such as Rue de Rome and the pedestrian precinct of Rue St Ferreo. And if you were intrigued by the *santons* in the Maison Diamantée, the traditional art of producing these regional painted-clay figurines is still carried on at Les Ateliers Marcel Carbonel at 47 Rue Neueve Sainte Catherine. The markets too are worth a visit, especially the improvised fish market on Quai des Belges most mornings and the remarkable garlic market in Course Belsunce (you'd never believe there were so many varieties!).

Theatre

Theatre buffs will want to seek out Marcel Maréchal's famous Théâtre de la Criée on the Quai de Rive Neuve or see one of Roland Petit's ballets. There are also fifteen other *théâtres* and an opera house in the city.

Sports and Recreation

The main beaches are the Plages du Prado to the east of the city along the splendid waterfront drive of the Corniche President J.F.Kennedy and facing the handsome Avenue du Prado. Information on tennis, golf, watersports, fishing, boat hire etc can be obtained from the Office du Tourisme.

Accommodation
The city boasts two 4-star hotels, the Pullman Beauvau (tel 91 54 91 00) at 4 Rue Beauvau in the Vieux Port and the Concorde-Prado (91 76 51 11) at 11 Avenue de Mazargues in the Prado quarter, but there are plenty of cheaper ones in areas off the Canebière. (However, tourists are advised to steer clear of the old town as this is reputed to be unsafe.) You can even stay in the hotel inside Le Corbusier's Cité Radieuse if the mood takes you.

Restaurants
For those with a large appetite and an unconstrained budget the famous Marseilles *bouillabaisse* fish stew is a must. Containing at least four of a possible eight varieties of fish and shellfish (including conger eel and optionally, lobster), cooked with saffron, garlic, fennel, onions and potatoes, and served with a red mayonnaise sauce you stir in known as *rouille*, it is indeed a classic meal. Members of the Guild of the Bouillabaisse Marseillaise in the Vieux Port include Le Cariobou (tel 91 33 23 94), 38 Place Thiers and Le Miramar (tel 91 91 10 40) at 12 Quai du Port, but the harbour area and the district behind Quai de Rive-Neuve abounds in restaurants so there is plenty of choice. Look out too for couscous restaurants and pizzerias (and, yes, there is a McDonald's). For a filling lunch try also the regional speciality snack of the *pan bagnat* – a six-inch-diameter bap filled with, effectively, a *salade niçoise* (13–20F). Though *sandwichs* (baguettes with a variety of fillings) and hot dogs (a great improvement on the US variety) are also good value at around 10F. However, those in search of wholemeal bread will have to look hard.

Excursions from Marseilles
For many holidaymakers in France the chief attraction of Marseilles is as the starting point for the Mediterranean coast, going eastwards towards the Riviera proper. There was a time when, using the local trains or the roads, one could make a leisurely journey from the *calanques* or fjords immediately east of Marseilles, by way of Cassis, La Ciotat, Les Lecques, Bandol, Sanary, Hyères, Le Lavandou, Cavalière, Cavalaire and St Tropez to St Raphael, before plunging into the traditional Riviera. And there was a time when this trip was rewarded with successive holidays in any of these places – smallish, comparatively unspoiled fishing villages or resorts. Some of them now, alas, have spread all over the place, their populations monstrously swollen during the season, their former charm hidden under massive blocks and commercial developments.

None the less, all is not yet lost. The coast is still incomparable over great stretches, and the hinterland is not yet totally over-grown by buildings and petrol stations. Some of the smaller places have suffered far more than others; some still have the magic of an earlier Mediterranean world.

Cassis

There was a time when Cassis, the first fishing-port-cum-holiday-resort east of Marseilles, was precisely that: a fairly busy little port where people from Marseilles and a reasonable number of other French holidaymakers came to relax and drink the delicious white wine which is grown in the hills.

Later came a casino, blocks of flats and more concrete. Today there is a permanent population of about 5000 with a holiday population of something like 20,000 at the peak of the season. However, most of the attractive physical features of Cassis are still more or less intact: the old château and remains of the ramparts, the lively port and the sharp hills behind the splendidly southern Place Pierre Baragnon (where you will find the 2-star Syndicat d'Initiative (tel 42 01 71 17)). Cap Canaille, the highest cliff in Europe (416 m/1364 ft) still rounds off the view superbly, and there are always the *calanques* of Port-Miou, En-Vau and Port-Pin, those curious Mediterranean fjords.

For those arriving by train (25 min from Marseilles) be warned – the town itself is 4 km (3 miles) from the station, there is no bus and taxis are very thin on the ground. The stationmaster will also charge you 12F per item for storing luggage as there are no automatic lockers (usually 3F unless of complicated electronic variety).

The first thing the traveller from Marseilles notices is the tremen-dous noise of cicadas in the pine trees, the almost complete absence of dark-skinned North Africans on the streets and the abundance of topless women sunbathers on the small sand-and-shingle beach.

Les Calanques

The main tourist attractions are the nearby *calanques* which Cassis claims as its own. And indeed it is considerably cheaper to explore these inlets from here (30–35F) than from Marseilles (85F). There is even a special trimaran submarine with glass observation panels, the *Aquascope*, which operates from the Quai des Baux (adults 50F, children 25F, duration 30 min). And the Kayak Club des Calanques, 11 Ave Viguerie hires out canoes for individual and group outings from 50F (1 hr) to 250F (daytrip including meal). The town also has a free museum and hosts a variety of cultural events (theatre, music, exhibitions etc) throughout the year (details from the SI).

Sports and Recreation
For the sports enthusiast Cassis has much to offer. There are clubs for skin-diving (3), sailing and wind-surfing (3), tennis (2) and horseriding (1) and plenty of opportunities for rock-climbing, mountain-bike rides and hill-walking. There is also an annual marathon from Marseilles (10,000 runners in 1988) in October and the tourist office organizes a number of minibus excursions in the surrounding area.

Accommodation and Restaurants
The hotels are still led – for old-timers – by the 3-star Roches Blanches (tel 42 01 09 30) in Ave des Calanques, and the more modest Le Commerce (tel 42 01 09 10) is still there, though the busy Berthe of an earlier day no longer goes from table to table with a huge tureen of soup (1-star, Boulevard Jean-Jaurès). The only other 3-star hotels are La Plage du Bestouan (tel 42 01 05 70), La Rade (tel 42 01 02 97) and Les Jardins du Campanile (42 01 84 85). Campers and caravanners should head for Les Cigales campsite (tel 42 01 07 34) in Ave de la Marne to the north of the town (open 15 Mar–15 Nov). The town plan available at the SI lists 34 restaurants in addition to those attached to hotels, so there is plenty of choice. And do ask for the wine, they are very proud of it.

La Ciotat

La Ciotat, 10 km (6 miles) east of Cassis, has a long and honourable industrial (ship-building) history. It has also the natural dignity of an old sea-coast settlement that bears the magnificently simple name of 'The City' (*ciotat-ciudad-civitas*), sheltered by the cape known as the Bec de l'Aigle, 'the eagle's beak'. Today La Ciotat has more than 30,000 residents – 60,000 in August. There is provision for most kinds of holidaymaker and no lack of entertainment and interest, including delightful excursions both seawards and inland.

Indeed, now that the shipyards have closed down (though the gigantic tower cranes still loom over the Vieux Port) the town has become very consciously geared towards tourism and the smart new air-conditioned tourist office (now upgraded to 3-star status) situated on the Boulevard Anatole France near the old harbour has a wealth of information to offer (tel 42 08 61 32).

Coastal Provence

The approach by train (10 min from Cassis) is again hampered by the fact that the town centre is 5 km (3 miles) from the station, but there is a regular bus service (4.50F single) from the forecourt that runs down the main beach areas before stopping at the SI. If arriving by car the A50 loops round the town with the Betelle Autoroute and the CD 559 feeding into the centre from the west and east respectively.

Cradle of the Cinema

La Ciotat is currently being promoted heavily as 'La Ville des Lumières' as it was here that the Lumière brothers, Louis and Auguste, presented to the world the first ever cinema show on 21 September 1895 (a commemorative monument stands on Bvd Beaurivage, Le Complexe Lumière has three screens and a theatre, and there is an annual film festival in June). Originally a Greek settlement dating from the 4th century BC, La Ciotat was much admired by the poet Lamartine and Stendhal, and in more recent times it gained fame as the birthplace of the *boules* variant known as *pétanque* (where tossing the metal balls is allowed but moving the feet is forbidden) in 1910. The cubist George Braques also lived here for a number of years.

With your back to the cranes the old harbour is very attractive and as well as a number of 17th-century churches there is a museum of local history. The narrow lanes in the old town are also a pleasant place to wander, and, to while away a hot afternoon watching the world drift by, a cool *kir* sitting outside the Bar d'Horloge in the Rue des Combattants is as good an idea as any. But the main attraction of La Ciotat now is as a leisure resort, with 6 km (4 miles) of sand-and-pebble beaches along the 'Golfe d'Amour', numerous sports stadia, tennis clubs, yachting, wind-surfing etc (details from the SI). The Parc du Mugel, however, has been kept as a nature reserve (Bec de l'Aigle, open daily except December).

Accommodation and Restaurants

The three main hotels (all 3-star) are Le King (tel 42 83 14 59) on Ave de St Jean, Mapotel Miramar (42 83 09 54) at 3 Bvd Beaurivage and the Ciotel le Cap (tel 42 83 90 30) on the Corniche

Opposite:	*Provençal bullfight, Palavas. The bull is not killed (top)*
	Aigues Mortes, a 13th-century walled town (below)
Overleaf:	*The Roman Aqueduct, the Pont du Gard, near Nîmes (top)*
	Gordes on the Vaucluse Plateau (below)

du Lionquet, all of which have restaurants. A list of 33 other restaurants, plus cafés, bars and sundry eating places, can be obtained from the SI together with a list of campsites, caravan parks and bungalows for rent.

St Cyr-les-Lecques

Between La Ciotat and Bandol is St Cyr-les-Lecques (or Les Lecques-St Cyr if you are a citizen of Les Lecques), which consists of the commune of St Cyr-sur-Mer and the bathing resorts of Les Lecques and La Madrague, which occupy the angles of a triangular plain dominated by wooded hills alongside a 2 km (1½ mile) stretch of fine sand shelving gently to the sea. The normal population of 5000 grows at the peak of the holiday season to 25,000, for whom there is everything that sun, sand, sea and the surrounding countryside can offer, including some very pleasant Côtes de Provence wines. La Cadière-Azur, 5 km (3 miles) inland on a hill with fine views, has a very enjoyable all-purpose red wine, *Cadièrienne*, along with its other attractions, though the autoroute from Bandol, which cuts a swathe through the valley below Cadière, is still a cause of concern to some villagers and visitors. For lovers of watersports there is the Aqualand leisure centre on the D559 towards La Ciotat with 15m (49 ft)-high toboggan slides etc. (June–Sept, no dogs).

Bandol

Bandol, 19 km (12 miles) east of La Ciotat, is the next coastal stop on the N559 from Marseilles. It is a very pleasant, old-established holiday resort that attracted discriminating British visitors long before the mass migrations began.

With a population of 6700 that rises to 35,000 during the summer months, in Bandol the visitor gets a first taste of what the Côte d'Azur proper has to offer. For here are moored some very large motor cruisers and the seafront restaurants and esplanades have a slightly more refined feel. The harbour is a 10 min walk from the railway station (12 min from La Ciotat by rail) and the Pavilion du Tourisme (tel 94 29 41 35) is on the Allée Alfred Vivien in the port

Previous page: *Aven Armand Grotto in the Causses (top right)*
The Gorge of Galamus in the Corbières (top left)
Roussillon's Côte Vermeille (below)
Opposite: *St Michel-de-Cuxa Abbey and Canigou Massif in*
Roussillon (top)
Château Royale at Collioure, Roussillon (below)

itself. The central square is the cool, plane-shaded Place de la Liberté with its fountain and adjacent bar, and a number of the narrow backstreets running parallel to the seafront have been designated *zone piétonne* for casual strolls. There is a Cultural Centre in the Rue Pons and a zoo and exotic gardens to the east of the town on autoroute B52. Celebrated residents have included Thomas Mann and Bertolt Brecht.

Sports and Recreation
Bandol is well equipped for indoor and outdoor sports and recreation with a casino, football stadium, boxing, tennis and sailing clubs, a fitness centre and a mini-golf course. And further attractions (including an art gallery and wine museum) can be found on Paul Ricard's Island of Bendor just off the coast. For those interested in motor-racing there is the Ricard *autodrome* on the N8 north of Le Castellet – home of the French Grand Prix since 1985 (nearby is the OK Corral amusement park).

Accommodation and Restaurants
Bandol has an impressive array of hotels, headed by the 4-star Pullman Ile Rousse (tel 94 29 46 86). There are also a number of 3-star establishments – including two, the Delos Palais (tel 94 32 22 23) and the Soukana (tel 94 32 22 23) on Bendor – and almost a score of other accredited lodging-houses. There are also 40 restaurants and crêperies, 17 of which are members of the Bandol Groupement des Hôteliers, and a similar number of bars and *glaciers.* Bandol, like Cassis, also produces a very acceptable wine in the 50 vineyards behind the town, some of which may be visited (list supplied by SI).

Sanary

9 km (6 miles) on from Bandol is Sanary, or, to give it its full title, Sanary-sur-Mer-Ollioules, a seaside town whose 11,700 population increases to 40,000 in the season. It is an attractive bathing resort, still with its charming small Mediterranean port nucleus tucked away in the shelter of the Gulf of St Nazaire and sheltered from the north by a range of hills. (The town's name derives from a corruption of 'St Nazaire'.) Sanary is well served for communications, with the B52 autoroute running to the north and the railway station just below it. The SI (tel 94 74 01 04) is in Jardin de Ville near the port itself.

Historically, Sanary has much to offer: an 11th-century Saracen tower; ruins of a feudal chateau; Roman remains; old houses in the upper village; a 16th-century chapel and fine views from Le

Gros Cerveau and Cap Gros. Excursions can be made to Port Issol, the Red Rocks, Bendor Island and Le Brusc, and inland to the villages of Cadière-Azur, Castellet and Le Beausset. The daily market is also no small part of a do-it-yourself holiday here and the exotic gardens and zoo (already mentioned under Bandol) are not far away. (Aldous Huxley used to live in Sanary.)

Accommodation
13 hotels are listed in the SI's useful leaflet, headed by the 3-star Hostellerie Berard (tel 94 29 31 43) in the Rue G.Peri in neighbouring Le Beausset, and there are a number of restaurants both on the beaches and inland.

Ile des Embiez

Just off the coast not far from Sanary (15 min boat service from Le Brusc) is the 95-hectare (235-acre) island of Embiez, home of the Paul Ricard Oceanographic Foundation whose aquaria etc have received over 100,000 visitors per year since it opened in 1973. The main hub of the island is the port of St Pierre des Embiez which has berths for 600 boats, and the resident yacht club hosts a number of international competitions etc. Apart from some fine beaches the island also has a football stadium, tennis courts, a 3-star hotel (the Helios), pinewoods and vineyards.

Six-Fours-les-Plages on the mainland nearby has a population of over 25,000 and a number of sandy beaches. There are eight hotels and two campsites. Details of sports etc can be obtained from the SI (tel 94 34 93 79) at Plage de Bonnegrâce.

Toulon

Toulon has the fascination of all great naval bases (it is France's principal one), but to the intriguing separateness of the no-entry zones is added a great deal of charm, elegance and, indeed, oddity. The massive re-building operations since the Second World War seem to have lifted some of the heaviness and blankness that tend to haunt the memory of those who knew the city between the wars.

With one of the finest harbours in the world and a normal population of 185,000, rising to 300,000 in the holiday season, Toulon is the southernmost city on the Côte d'Azur and, within the shelter of the surrounding hills, averages something like 290 days of sunshine a year. With its nearby beaches and countryside, and the wider choice bigger towns always offer in shops, hotels

Coastal Provence

and restaurants, it is a much better bet for the holidaymaker than many of the smaller, highly advertised centres.

Artists and tourists alike are re-discovering the advantages Toulon offers. With the slopes of Mont Faron immediately behind the city and the Gros Cerveau 40 km (25 miles) to the west, Toulon is also within easy reach of St Mandrier, Le Brusc, Sanary, Bandol, and St Cyr-les-Lecques. There are also regular bus and train services along the coast from Marseilles and St Raphael with further links eastward to Menton and the Italian frontier. In addition, there is an airport, Aéroport Toulon-Hyères, 18 km (12 miles) from the city centre. The main tourist office (tel 94 22 08 22) is situated at 8 Ave Colbert near the railway station but if this is closed (eg on Bastille Day) then it is worth knowing that there is an annexe in the station itself that is usually open (tel 94 62 73 87).

Toulon's fame dates back to Roman times when it was the centre for producing the purple dye used to colour imperial togas known as Toulon Purple. In more recent times it was here that the then obscure artillery captain Napoleon Bonaparte first made his name against the English in 1793. And during the Second World War the Roads were the scene of one of the biggest scuttling operations of all time when the French Mediterranean Fleet of 60 ships was deliberately sunk to prevent it falling into German hands. (The French novelist George Bernanos also wrote a number of his books whilst in Toulon.)

Sightseeing
As might be expected in a naval city, considerable interest is focussed on the ports, both the old (Darse Vieille) and the new. Between the restaurants spread along the Quai Stalingrad may be seen the famous Atlantes by Puget supporting the balcony of the Town Hall and if the US 6th Fleet is in you may be lucky enough to be entertained by their band as you watch the sun set over the harbour. Further inland, in the Place Victor Hugo, is the impressive 19th-century opera house and nearby is the Place Puget – another congregating area for locals and tourists alike – with its ancient dolphin fountain now renowned for the creeper that completely obscures the sculpture. Indeed Toulon is well endowed with fountains, a particularly ornate example being in the Place de la Liberté, scene of wild street-dancing on Bastille Day. Also worth seeing are the great gateway of the arsenal and other magnificent surviving gates. There are seven fine collections of art, ethnography and social and architectural history in addition to the great Naval Museum, the Cathedral, the 17th-

century Fort St Louis at Mourillon, and every opportunity for entertainment, music and film-going during the season.

A little road train, the *Tchou...Tchou* (Quai Stalingrad, Apr–Sept) makes a circuit of the old town and the beaches at Mourillon if you want to save shoe leather, and there is even a night-train (Jul–Aug, 08.30–23.00, duration 15 min) which, though no doubt fun, can be disturbing if you happen to be staying in a hotel on its route.

Mont Faron
Particularly recommended is the *téléphérique* trip up Mt Faron (493 m/1617 ft) to the north of the city (from Bvd Perrichi). The cable car only takes 6 min to reach the top and the views both of Toulon with its monster warships moored outside and the surrounding valleys and hills are stunning. As well as a bar and two restaurants there is also a museum dedicated to the 1944 Allied landings at the summit and another *Tchou...Tchou* will take you to the chapel in a converted *poudrière* and the zoo if you wish (adults 15F, children 10F return). Pleasanter still, however, is to wander through the 103 hectares (254 acres) of pine trees and bleached rocks, gazing across the valleys on the far side whilst strange butterflies flutter past and the cicadas' thrumming echoes all round.

Accommodation and Restaurants
Central Toulon has three 3-star hotels – the Hôtel Altea Tour Blanche (tel 94 24 41 57) in Bvd Admiral Vence, Le Grand Hôtel (tel 94 22 59 50) at 4 Place de la Liberté and SARL La Corniche (tel 94 41 35 12) at 1 Littoral Frédéric Mistral in the Mourillon district – but a list of others as well as a great many restaurants (with their specialities) can be obtained from the SI. If you've yet to try it, *soupe au pistou*, made from five different varieties of haricot bean, is a regional delicacy to be savoured (but remember that many restaurants don't usually start serving evening meals until about 20.00).

Sports and Recreation
There are a great number of sports clubs and associations in Toulon, from *musculation* to *parachutisme,* and a thick booklet covering all can be obtained from the SI. (For rugby fans, the Toulon Rouges et Noirs won the French championships in 1987.) There are also Olympic swimming-pools and ample yachting facilities. The main beaches are at Mourillon to the east of the city.

A word of warning. Traffic flow, or *circulation* as the French have

109

it (though in most great cities today there is little evidence of either 'flow' or 'circulation'), can be a major obstacle to using Toulon as a holiday base during the peak months. Traffic along the main coast roads can become a nightmare at times, and though, if one has time, one can always take to the hills to bypass some of the worst bottlenecks, even this is not altogether the answer at certain times of the year, particularly if you are not a totally relaxed, calm and naturally first-class driver with a head for heights and bends.

This is one of the reasons for making the most of Toulon itself, with its inexhaustible interest and animation, the splendid views from its terraced surroundings, and the wealth of history and folklore in its naval and military establishments, ancient prison and its inevitable sea legends. One of the latter tells of the *Patte-Luzerne* (she is also sometimes called the *Gallipetun*), a ship so huge that her stern had hardly cleared the Toulon roadstead when her bows were already emerging west of the Straits of Gibraltar...her decks were covered with cornfields, vineyards and grazing land with abundant cattle, and her masts were so tall that the boys who climbed to the mast-top had white hair and beards by the time they came down on deck again.

Hyères

Continuing eastward from Toulon the first port of call on the coast road is Hyères and the Giens Peninsula, with the islands of Porquerolles, Port Cros and the Levant.

Hyères, which normally has 42,000 inhabitants and three times as many in August, has been a celebrated resort since the 18th century: it is at once the oldest and the most southerly holiday resort on the Côte d'Azur. The older parts of the town are terraced on the slopes of Castéou Hill (204 m/670 ft), the modern districts are mainly in the plain. It has retained a surprising amount of charm in the face of the onslaught of urban development and mass holidaymaking, and even during a casual drive through the town, busy as it may be, a feeling of quiet grace, ancient depths and elegance persists. On a tour of the coast from Marseilles to Menton visitors will find that Hyères is one of the places whose flavour has been least affected by undesirable change. Like Menton, it has one of the best climates in the whole of France, and it is still a town to stroll in, either to the fortress on the hill or through the picturesque old streets that radiate from it. The handsome, tree-lined streets of the modern town are no less pleasant to walk in: the modern ant-column of tourists along the

Côte seems, without actually doing so, to slow down a little as it passes through Hyères. The 3-star Syndicat d'Initiative is in the Place G.Clemenceau.

Le Fenouillet

The reassuring charm of parts of Hyères itself is a personal and subjective experience. The actual attractions of its surrounds are safer ground for the writer who would like you to enjoy what he has enjoyed. Le Fenouillet, for example, offers a pleasant excursion (it can be done comfortably on foot from the old town within two hours, there and back). Le Fenouillet (about 300 m/984 ft) is the summit of the little Maurettes range which runs from east to west above Hyères. The view from the top is well worth the effort.

Beaches

The principal beaches are at L'Ayguade (4 km/3 miles); Hyères-Plage, a really fine sandy beach (6 km/4 miles); La Capte, on the eastern side of the Giens Peninsula (8 km/5 miles); and at L'Almanarre (5 km/3 miles) on the road from Hyères to Toulon by way of Carqueiranne.

The Giens Peninsula

From the town of Hyères to Giens, at the end of the peninsula of that name, there is also much of interest. The salt-marshes (Salins des Pesquiers) were formerly *étangs* (land-locked pools) which were extensively fished: the salt-workings were established in 1850. The lagoon, of which the salt-marshes were once part, separates the two sandy stretches of the peninsula and there are fine views from the Madrague road which runs along the northern coast of the western tip of the peninsula. The village of Giens, which stands on a hill, also offers extensive and beautiful views of coast and sea. At the eastern tip of the peninsula stands La Tour Fondue, a fortress which guards the passage between the mainland and Porquerolles and is the embarkation point for the Golden Isles.

Accommodation

Hyères has four 3-star hotels, including the Hôtel Bona on the Plage de l'Hippodrome (tel 94 58 00 85) and Le Paris at 20 Ave de Belgique (tel 94 65 33 61) and about 30 other establishments (there are also three more 3-star establishments in Giens).

Isles d'Hyères

The group of islands off the Giens Peninsula, the Iles d'Hyères – or, as they are sometimes called, the Iles d'Or (Golden Isles) –

Coastal Provence

consists of Porquerolles (7 km/4½ miles long and about 2 km/ 1½ miles wide), Port-Cros (4½ km/3 miles long, about 2 km/ 1½ miles wide) and the Isle du Levant (8 km/5 miles long but less than 1¼ km/1 mile wide). Porquerolles is accessible from La Tour Fondue (20 min), Toulon (90 min), Le Lavandou (90 min), and from Cavalaire by arrangment. Port-Cros and Ile du Levant are accessible from various points on the Giens Peninsula and from Cavalaire, Le Lavandou and Toulon. Detailed information about the islands is obtainable from the Sydicat d'Initiative at Hyères. Accommodation in the islands is, in fact, quite limited, so unless you can afford to pay top prices at the last minute make your reservations as early as possible.

Porquerolles
Porquerolles is one of the most attractive islands off the coast, with rocky coves, tiny creeks, beaches of fine sand and comparative solitude over much of the island. It contains relics of Ligurians, Celts, Etruscans, Greeks (Phocaeans), Romans and Saracens. St Honorat spent some years here before founding his hermitage on the Lerins Islands, off Cannes (AD 375), and it is believed to have been the refuge both of the troubadour Rimbaud d'Orange – who is said to have celebrated in too precise terms the charms of Queen Marguerite, the wife of Louis IX (St Louis) – and of the Man in the Iron Mask while he was in transit between the Château d'If and Ste Marguerite, in the Lerins.

The small port and village of Porquerolles are pleasant. Some years ago a visitor wrote: 'In the interior of the island there are few inhabitants, pinewoods, vineyards and an abundance of African-type vegetation.' This flavour of the island is still there, though somewhat modified. Most of the area of Porquerolles was taken under the protection of the State in 1971. There are five hotels, one of which, Le Mas du Langoustier (tel 94 58 30 09), is a 3-star establishment.

Port-Cros
The island of Port-Cros has only one hotel, the 3-star Le Manoir d'Hélène (tel 94 05 90 52), and is regarded by its devotees as the most beautiful of the three islands, with a more rugged profile, rising higher from the sea, and with richer greenery than the others.

Ile du Levant
The Ile du Levant is best known as one of the favourite spots on the Mediterranean for naturists, who can enjoy the sun in natural nudity undisturbed (there are three hotels, headed by the 2-star Heliotel (tel 94 05 90 63)).

Hyères to St Raphael

From Hyères to St Raphael is a stretch of coast which includes some of France's best-known resorts, backed by the beautiful hinterland of the Maures Massif. Some of the resorts have grown so much in the past few decades as to have become almost unrecognizable while others have survived the tourist *putsch* with less obvious damage. But the core of each is still there to be found and the coast between them still has interludes of great and comparatively unspoiled natural beauty.

Le Lavandou

Le Lavandou, which some people thought they had discovered in the 1930s, was a thriving fishing village in the 14th century, and was visited in 1537 by Rabelais on his way to the Ile du Levant. Sheltered by the Pierre d'Avenoun and the Maures Massif, with one of the finest beaches of the whole coast and other good beaches within easy reach, Le Lavandou, 23 km (14 miles) east of Hyères, was at one time noted for its uncrowded sands and tiny, rather smart village and pricey small shops. Today its basic population is still no more than 4300 or so, but now it has to provide for a July–August influx of something like 50,000. The SI is on the Quai Baptistin Pins.

Accommodation
The built-up area has been formidably extended and the wide range of hotels varies from the 4-star Le Club de Cavalière (tel 94 05 80 14) and no less than 12 3-star establishments to many modest places at the other end of the scale, along with the now almost inevitable motel. Campsites, of course, account for much of the growing summer population. The hinterland is superb, with the Forest of the Dom and the villages of Gassin and Ramatuelle within easy reach, and miles of cork and chestnut woods. The southern vegetable soup, *soupe au pistou,* is particularly good here.

Excursions
A pleasant excursion from Le Lavandou, by way of Bormes-les-Mimosas through the heavily wooded mountains round Collobrières, includes the village of St Guillaume (5 km/3 miles from Collobrières on a good road); the Maures peak of La Sauvette (a 4-hour trek there and back on foot); Notre Dame des Anges (4 hours there and back on foot, about an hour there and back by car) and, perhaps most interesting of all, to the Charterhouse of La Verne.

The Charterhouse of La Verne

This superb ruin, situated in one of the loneliest and most beautiful parts of the Maures range, was founded in the 12th century on the northern slope of a ridge between the Verne River and the Mole Valley. The buildings were restored in the 18th century but abandoned after the French Revolution. You can reach it by a forest road from the D14 (Collobrières-Grimaud) at a point about 6 km (4 miles) east of Collobrières. Until recently the last 3 km (2 miles) had to be completed on foot but now cars can drive right up to the monastery. The magnificent remaining masses of ancient stonework, spread out over their mountain eyrie, have a splendid main entrance in serpentine stone with a beautiful small cloister of the same materials. The views from the site are breathtaking, and in the season the custodians of the building provide simple refreshments of bread, cheese and wine. A pleasant way back to Bormes is by the Col de Babaou, along which it is worth keeping a weather eye open on your left for an extraordinary Victorian-Gothic private chapel in the middle of the chestnut and cork woods: it stands out like a construction by the American artist Joseph Cornell.

Cavalière

Cavaliere, which is part of the commune of Le Lavandou, also has a fine, sandy beach in a setting of pinewoods, and although it must in the season take much of Le Lavandou's overspill, it gives the impression of being one of the less aggressively developed resorts. It has a few excellent hotels, details of which are obtainable from the Syndicat d'Initiative at Le Lavandou.

Le Rayol

Continuing eastwards, after Cavalière comes Le Rayol-Le Canadel-sur-mer, a cumbrous title for the coast at Canadel and the pleasant holiday resort of Le Rayol which faces the Isles d'Hyères. Le Canadel and Le Rayol between them have about ten hotels (including the 4-star Bailli de Suffren, which is on the sea at Le Rayol), good beaches, masses of flowers and wooded *calanques*, backed by the Pradels hills. Henry Royce, partner of C.S.Rolls and designer of many of the well-known cars that bore their joint names, once lived here.

Cavalaire

From Le Rayol to Cavalaire, the next resort, is still a beautiful coast drive. Cavalaire itself, though its population figures are comparable with those of Le Lavandou – amounting to just under 3000 normally, and about 40,000 in August – gives a much more discouraging impression of sheer size. This may be because it has 3 km (2½ miles) of beach, and the enormous amount of building that has gone on sprawls all over the place to make the most of the seafront. It certainly seems to be the most drastically developed of the smaller places.

But whatever Cavalaire has suffered aesthetically, many more thousands of people have had splendid holidays here than could have done years ago. With at least a score of hotels, many of them very good indeed, every facility the average holidaymaker needs, and such lovely old Provençal villages as Gassin, Ramatuelle and Grimaud within easy reach, it is not surprising that it now has a 2-star Syndicat d'Initiative (Square de Lattre-de-Tassigny) to help the ever-increasing tide of visitors.

From Cavalaire to St Tropez the way lies through La Croix-Valmer, in the vine-covered hills that shelter the bay of Cavalaire to the north, and then along the winding Col de Collebasse with fine views. Before taking the main N98 into St Tropez it would be well worth while having a look at the hill-village of Gassin, the ruined windmills of Paillas and, if you can so arrange your journey, the village of Grimaud. But these can also be conveniently visited from St Tropez if you decide to move in there first and stay for a while (see next chapter).

St Tropez

As the railway cuts inland between Toulon and St Raphael and cars and buses can take for ever in the crowded summer traffic, one of the simplest and arguably the best approach to St Tropez is by boat from St Raphael (80F return from Gare Maritime in the old port, duration 50 min). If you happen to have a private plane, of course, there is always the little aerodrome at St Tropez la Mole 16 km (10 miles) out of town. The small and very busy SI (tel 94 97 45 21) is on the Quai Jean-Jaurès in the Vieux Port.

St Tropez is a place of extraordinary contradictions. Sometimes described as a summer resort which has fairly recently become fashionable, its 'in' period was quite some time ago and it is regarded nowadays as trendy only in mass-circulation newspapers which are invariably many fashions out of date. It is also about the only resort on the Côte d'Azur which turns its back firmly on the Mediterranean and faces north. Its reputation as the favourite spot of 'the beautiful people' has resulted in its having

Coastal Provence

more spectators than spectacle, and it is hardly possible to see its originally beautiful waterfront for the bulbous and top-heavy 'luxury' yachts which have replaced the old fishing boats.

None the less, the features that first attracted celebrated holiday-makers are still here, if you dig for them. Much of the old town is charming, there are quiet corners away from the blatantly commercial quays, and the views inland towards the Maures and seaward over the old town from the Mole du Portalet are still fascinating. Its basic population of nearly 7000 is estimated to grow to 80,000 in the season – that is in July and August – but even during a weekend in June it can be as crowded as Brighton on a Bank Holiday. In recent times its famous residents have included Maupassant, Colette, Cocteau and Brigitte Bardot who immortalized it on screen in *And God Created Woman*. You may occasionally see a famous face, but most of them have found less exposed corners away from the port.

Torpes the Centurion
The town gets its name from Torpes, a centurion who was beheaded by order of Nero in AD68 for refusing to renounce his Christian faith. The body was then set adrift in an open boat with a dog and a cockerel on board and eventually arrived, miraculously untouched by the starving animals, at a fishing village which became known at first as St Torpes.

The Old Town
After the initial shock of the overcrowded port there are some delightful surprises round the corner, where you can eat in peace and even look out over a quiet few yards of beach with a working-boat lying by the wall. But these you must seek out for yourselves: it is well worth it. There is a superb serpentine doorway to the 18th-century church in the old town, and the chapel of Ste Anne, with its views over St Tropez and the gulf, is worth a visit (about a kilometre along the D93 southwards towards Pampelonne, plus a seven-minute climb on foot).

The Annonciade Museum behind the Quai de l'Epi has paintings and sculpture from 1890 to 1940 (including Matisse, Signac, Dufy and Braque), there is a naval museum in the massive Citadel overlooking the harbour (from the grounds of which are splendid views of the town and coastline) and wandering through the narrow streets of the old town is very pleasant. And when you are fed up with gazing at the enormous yachts moored in the harbour, the big flashy motorcycles cruising past and the ever-present scruffy poodles dangled by the more pretentious women, there are always the shady trees and the *pétanque* players in the Place des Lices until your boat comes in.

However, if you are shopping be warned, prices can be very high and, even for such mundane items as postcards, can vary enormously (the same card can be 18F at one end of the street and double that at the other). For a reasonably priced *espresso* try Bistro du Port on the corner of the Quai Gabriel Peri (4F at the bar – many charge 10F).

Festivals
St Tropez hosts festivals of all kinds, including two *bravades*, or pageants, one on 16, 17 and 18 May, the other – *Bravade des Espagnols* – on 15 June. These are associated more or less historically with the musketeers who tried to repel the pirates who attacked the town incessantly in the 15th century. The old Citadel, on its knoll to the east of the town, is the setting for the *Nuits de la Citadelle* in July and August. The town also hosts an international bridge festival (April) and a Rolls-Royce Rally (October).

Accommodation and Restaurants
There are four 4-star hotels in St Tropez itself – Le Byblos (tel 94 97 00 04) on Ave Paul Signac, La Bastide de St Tropez (tel 94 97 58 16) on Route des Carles, and Résidence de la Pinède (tel 94 97 04 21) and La Mandarine (tel 94 97 21 00) in the Bouillabaise and Tahiti beach areas, respectively. The SI has a list of others as well as 45 recommended restaurants both in St Tropez and the surrounding villages. There are also a number of campsites and caravan sites in the neighbouring region.

Sports and Recreation
Yachting, golf, aerobics, fishing, tennis, yoga etc are all catered for and the Moulin Blanc Sport Complex has a swimming-pool, two stadia, a sailing school, over 30 tennis courts, horseriding, a deep-sea diving school and many other facilities. The beaches, of course, are splendid – not only Pampelonne but also the Graniers, the Salins, the Bouillabaisse and others. Further details from the SI.

Excursions from St Tropez
St Tropez is within easy reach of many of the most beautiful of those inland attractions which can make you smile quietly to yourself when you hear people disparaging the Côte d'Azur who know only the overcrowded parts of its shoreline. Such attractions include Ramatuelle, Cogolin, Cap Camarat and the Chartreuse de la Verne. Cycles, scooters and motorbikes can be hired

from Rue Joseph Quaranta (off the Place des Lices). But be warned, though the rates are reasonable the deposits are high (eg daily 10-speed cycle hire 40F, deposit 500F) and make sure you check the opening hours (particularly at weekends) as they might not coincide with the departure times of your ferry back. A good daytrip by bike (low gears essential) is out along the D93 through the vineyards to the attractive hill-villages of Ramatuelle and Gassin, then take the D61 from Gassin which joins the D98A back along the coast to St Tropez (allow about two hours actual cycling and walking up steep hills in addition to your time in the villages themselves).

Ste Maxime

On the other side of the Gulf of St Tropez is Ste Maxime, which faces due south and attracts something like 35,000 visitors in the high summer. It has fine sand, 26 hotels including two in the 4-star category, and St Tropez across the gulf, either as an added attraction or as a place you would rather look at than stay in. The 2-star SI (tel 94 96 19 24) is in the Boulevard de la République.

Port Grimaud

Tucked away in the gulf is Port Grimaud, the creation of one man, François Spoerry. This lagoon village is similar in conception to the new resorts of Languedoc-Roussillon, in that it was built on a stretch of salt-marsh and sand-dunes. The houses are curiously pleasing and effective imitations of traditional Mediterranean, and the village has everything the yachtsman could want, including a number of good up-market restaurants. An English writer who has made a special study of the French Mediterranean harbours has called it 'a three-dimensional *trompe l'oeil* in good taste'. It is also expensive.

St Aygulf

The next stage of the journey east towards St Raphael – where, according to today's conventions, the French Riviera itself begins (and later joins its Italian counterpart at Ventimiglia) – is reached at St Aygulf, which is linked with Fréjus. The setting of St Aygulf is as attractive as only this coast can ensure, sheltered as it is with pinewoods and groves of oak and cork-oak. There is also a beach of fine sand, surrounded by rocks.

The extent to which St Aygulf has grown over recent years can be measured by the fact that its permanent population of 3000 or so goes up to nearly 40,000 in July and August. Much of this is accounted for by campers and caravanners, as it offers some of the best sites along the coast. There is also an adequate range of hotels and a Syndicat d'Initiative in Place de la Poste (tel 94 81 22 09) to cope with all enquiries. For sun, sea and sand, St Aygulf fills the bill: for other entertainment, night-life and cultural interests, Fréjus supplies the need, with Roman remains, cinemas and even *corridas*. Fréjus itself, which lies between the Maures range and the Esterel, and leads on to St Raphael, is best considered, however, as the introduction to the next chapter, the Riviera proper.

Antibes sea wall

Côte D'Azur

If you are concerned with saving time and effort, one way to reach the Riviera is to step into an aeroplane at London Airport on a dull, cool, cloudy, unappetizing London evening, and step out less than two hours later into the warm, flower-scented, star-filled, sea-sparkling night at Nice Airport.

However, the route along the coastline has much to offer and the *real* Riviera – the Côte d'Or proper of Cannes, Antibes, Juan-les-Pins, Nice, Monte Carlo and Monaco – has now pushed westwards and begins, effectively with the resorts of Fréjus and St Raphael.

Fréjus

Fréjus almost adjoins St Raphael, with which it is associated in most holidaymakers' minds. The city took its name from Forum

Julii, the oldest Roman town in Gaul (founded by Julius Caesar in 49BC) and is sometimes called the 'Pompeii of Provence' because of its Roman remains. It is certainly a worthy gateway to the most famous stretch of the whole French Mediterranean coast.

Fréjus – or, to give it its full name, Fréjus-Ville et Fréjus-Plage – is a town of 30,000 which grows to 100,000 in the season. Apart from its wide range of Roman remains – including an arena now mostly used for rock concerts and regular bullfights – it has a 13th-century cathedral, a 12th-century cloister and a 5th-century baptistery. With every kind of entertainment and sport for holidaymakers (including *corridas*), it is well situated where the Maures Massif gives way to the beautiful stretch known as the Esterel, and offers, among its many local attractions, excursions to Mont Vinaigre and the Pic de l'Ours (through the forest of the Esterel). Just outside the town there is also a Marine Corps museum and a 20-hectare (49-acre) zoological park at Le Capitou off the A8.

Fréjus-Ville is situated 2 km (1 mile) inland from the rather garish beach area, which merges with St Raphael at the eastern end, and has considerable charm – particularly around the Cathedral Close quarter where the old Roman port used to be (the sea has certainly receded considerably in the last two millennia). The Tourist Office (tel 94 51 54 14) is at 325 Rue Jean-Jaurès (there is also an SI (tel 94 51 53 87) in the Place Calvini and another (tel 94 51 48 42) on the Bvd de la Libération in Fréjus-Plage) and produces a helpful double-sided brochure (with street maps) jointly with St Raphael.

Accommodation and Restaurants
Fréjus-Ville and Fréjus-Plage share between them about two dozen hotels, with the 2-star Oasis (tel 94 51 50 44) on the beach itself. Camping and caravan sites are legion in the neighbourhood, and there are also other kinds of accommodation, such as youth hostels and holiday houses for families. For further details and a comprehensive list of restaurants pick up the brochure at the SI.

Sports and Recreation
Fréjus has an aero club and a number of sports clubs from *boules* and rowing to *cyclotourisme* and ramblers, and the Aquatica leisure complex on the N98 (towards Ste Maxime) promises fun for all the family (open June-Sept). There is also a go-kart track nearby. In the harbour at Fréjus-Plage (as, sporadically, elsewhere along the coast) there are also occasional water-jousts

involving two launches with combatants perched precariously on a raised platform at one end. The contestants invariably end up in the water (sometimes even before they raise their lances!).

St Raphael

St Raphael, 'gateway to the Esterel', once a smallish, elegant winter and summer resort, has grown during the past 20 years almost out of all recognition. This process has been aggravated by the fact that the town is situated at the point at which the bulk of the Riviera-bound traffic hits the coast, creating, at times, bottlenecks of world-championship calibre. It is ironical to recall that Alphonse Karr, the French journalist who put St Raphael on the map in the 1860s, took a house here because he had found this little corner of the coast quieter than Nice. It was not long before he was trying to persuade his friends – writers, painters and musicians – to join him. Earlier, in the 18th century, St Raphael became temporarily famous as the landing place of Napoleon Bonaparte's ships on their victorious return from Egypt. In 1814, Napoleon visited St Raphael again, only this time in defeat and on his way to exile in Elba. Other famous visitors have included Dumas, Maupassant and Berlioz who composed his opera *Romeo and Juliette* here in 1866.

The town's normal population of 27,000 goes up to 100,000 in August, and its 3-star Syndicat d'Initiative (tel 94 95 16 87) in the Place de la Gare is kept busy supplying information, advice and guidance. Arriving by train can be disappointing. Backpackers be warned – the *consignes* at the station get so busy in the holiday season that queuing until one becomes vacant is common. And the initial impact of crowded car-filled streets and uninspiring modern architecture can be depressing. But take heart, the sandy beaches are only a short walk away and the sea, if not crystal clear, is certainly warm and blue.

Sightseeing
The attractive 12th-century church built in the Romanesque-Provençal style is one of the few remaining buildings of historical interest in the town and used to dominate the old port. Sadly, however, it has now been all but completely obscured by recent property development, notably the casino. There is also a Museum of Underwater Archaeology which houses the finds of the local scuba-divers, particularly amphorae from nearby Roman Fréjus, the 'Pompeii of Provence'. But St Raphael has few pretentions in this direction – it is primarily a leisure resort. However, as

a base for exploring the great crags and ravines of the Esterel (1726 hectares/4265 acres) it is ideally situated. For hill-walkers the SI has a useful booklet, *Connaissance de l'Esterel*, which gives detailed walks (with maps) of 10, 15, 20 and 25 km (6, 10, 12 and 15 miles). Cycles, scooters etc can be hired from Patrick Moto at 280 Ave General Leclerc (cycles 40F per day, 800F deposit; 50cc 'scooters' 150F, 5000F deposit).

Accommodation and Restaurants

Here, and in the neighbouring Boulouris, accommodation is on the scale of a major resort. However, it is advisable to book in advance during the summer months as this is a very popular watering-hole. There are more than 60 hotels in and around St Raphael including four 3-star hotels in the town itself and five more in the neighbouring resorts of Boulouris, Le Dramont, Anthéor and St Aygulf (2). The SI can also provide a formidable list of letting agencies and eight camping/caravan sites are listed in the Fréjus/St Raphael brochure.

Sports and Recreation

In a town that is dedicated to leisure it is not surprising that St Raphael and its fellow resorts are well endowed with facilities. 'Drop anchor at St Raphael' invites one leaflet from the SI which describes anchorages for over 2500 boats (space for 1800 at the newly opened Port Santa Lucca alone) along the 43 km (27 miles) of beaches and *calanques*. There are also 50 all-year tennis courts and two 18-hole golf courses as well as kayaks, horseriding and most other leisure activities – in addition to the casino, five discotheques and three cinemas. The SI has a thick brochure (*Sports Loisirs*) listing all the possibilities with a detailed plan of where they are situated.

Agay

The next resort, going east along the N98 coast road (the Corniche d'Or, or Corniche of the Esterel, which runs from St Raphael to La Napoule and then rejoins the N7), is Agay. Over-looked by the ridge of the Rastel (over 300 m/984 ft), Agay is situated in the heart of the red cliffs, classical pines and azure sea section of the coast. Along this stretch every resort has a beautiful setting, marred only by indiscriminate development here and there along the coast roads and the apparently inevitable pollution problems of a tideless sea liable to be contaminated by both human waste and oil. There are five 2-star hotels including the Esterella (tel 94 44 00 58).

Anthéor

Even more dramatically pictorial is the next resort, Anthéor, where the red rocky cliffs are deeply indented by the sea. Anthéor-Plage, which is part of the Commune of St Raphael, is set against the backcloth of Cap Roux and the wooded hills of the Esterel. Accommodation at Anthéor-Plage itself is comparatively limited (there are only two hotels, both 2-star), but there is a camping/caravan site.

Le Trayas

Le Trayas, 9 km (6 miles) farther east, is in terraces at the foot of the Esterel and has particularly attractive beaches of sand and shingle, surrounded by rocks, at La Figueirette and Notre Dame. The only hotel is the 2-star Relais des Calanques (tel 94 44 14 06).

Théoule

From Le Trayas the road goes round the headland known as the Pointe de l'Esquillon by way of Miramar to Théoule. Théoule is a thriving holiday centre which has grown rapidly from a tiny, semi-circular beach with two or three shops, one small hotel – the 2-star Corniche d'Or (tel 93 75 00 23), which serves excellent fish soup – and one expensive hotel with its own tiny bay, to become a very popular resort with several good hotels (one 4-star), excellent beaches and a starred Syndicat d'Initiative.

Mandelieu-La-Napoule

A little farther on is La Napoule-Plage, or, to give it its official name, Mandelieu-La-Napoule, a town with a population of over 14,000. This resort has over 20 starred hotels (including the 4-star Ermitage du Riou (tel 93 49 95 56) and the 4-star plus Hôtel Loews-La Napoule (tel 93 49 90 00)), sandy beaches on the sea and on the River Siagne, art exhibitions, every kind of water-sport and recreation (including Mandelieu race-course) and Cannes within easy reach (8 km/5 miles). The setting of La Napoule is attractive, lying as it does at the foot of the rock of San Peyre (about 140 m/459 ft), and there is a château with 14th-century towers. This was restored in 1919 by Henry Clews, an American sculptor, and now contains the La Napoule Henry Clews Memorial Art Foundation, with works by the donor. Nearly 50 restaurants are listed in the guide available from the SI (tel 93 49 95 31) in the Ave Henry Clews. It also gives details of campsites, sports, exhibitions, etc.

Cannes

An early guidebook to Cannes said that it owed its success to the beauty of its situation, the mildness of its climate and the magnificence of the festivals held there. It also described the town, quoting an unnamed source, as 'the winter salon of the world's aristocracy'.

That was quite a few years ago. Today its year-round population is over 72,000, swollen to double that figure in July and August. It has an International Film Festival, a Festival of Amateur Films, a Festival of Advertising Films and many other festivals related mainly to the business side of pop music, television and other commercial arts. It also has an international fireworks festival. However, despite such outside incursions it has retained many of its own local customs, including the 'Battle of the Flowers' display, various regattas, and (not to be missed) some intensely local and deep-rooted celebrations which take place on and around the dramatic hill, Mont Chevalier (also known as the Colline du Suquet) which dominates the old port and what remains of the old town. Among the best-known and one of the most beautiful of these local events is the Mimosa Festival in February. Curiously enough, mimosa was first imported to Cannes as comparatively recently as 1835: today about 1500 acres (607 hectares) are devoted to its cultivation, mainly for export.

Cannes has, naturally, one of the best-equipped Syndicats d'Initiative (4 stars) in the Palais des Festivals et des Congrès, La Croisette (tel 93 39 24 53) (there is also one above the railway station (tel 93 99 19 77)). It has also, in addition to high-speed links with Nice airport, regular shipping-line services to New York, Central and Southern America and the main Mediterranean ports.

Lord Brougham

Cannes acquired its English popularity when, in 1834, Lord Brougham, then Britain's Chancellor of the Exchequer, was on his way to Nice and discovered that a cholera epidemic in Provence had closed the frontier at the River Var. As a result, Brougham turned back and decided to spend his holiday in Cannes, then little more than a small fishing port. He liked it so much that he returned there every winter for 34 years, and was gradually joined by most of the English aristocracy, including the Prince of Wales (later Edward VII), who became a regular visitor. Other celebrated former residents include the peripatetic Maupassant and the Provençal poet Frédéric Mistral (the publisher Barley Alison was also born here).

Côte D'Azur

Le Suquet

The town itself was named after the reeds (*cannes*) that once grew in the marshes around the foot of Mont Chevalier/Le Suquet which was later crowned by a fortified tower to defend the abbots of Lérins and the fisherfolk against the Saracens.

Those who still like to imagine what the old Cannes was like will be drawn to Mont Chevalier, with its 17th-century church of Notre-Dame de l'Esperance and the square tower and other relics of the ancient château of the abbots. The views from the hill are superb, particularly on festival nights.

Of course, the amount of building and development has changed the character of Cannes as a whole, but there are still quiet corners and there is more than enough in the way of music and entertainment all the year round for the growing numbers of middle-aged and elderly French people who are making it their permanent home.

Beaches

There are plenty of highly organized beaches in Cannes: 27 in all, of which 7 are public. Palm Beach has its world-famous Casino, and the promenade and beaches of La Croisette extend for almost 2 km (1 mile), from the gardens of the Municipal Casino to Palm Beach Casino and the Cap de la Croisette. If you find the beaches crowded, and the spectacle less elegant than you had imagined, content yourself with enjoying the magnificent seaward view and the cluster of the old town – as someone once wrote, it is perhaps better to live opposite a beautiful view than in it. The harbours are now so well geared to the pleasure-yacht business that the sybarite hardly needs to leave his floating home except for an evening on the town, and as for coping with the short-based waves and sudden bad-tempered outbursts of the off-shore Mediterranean, he can leave that to the hardier spirits.

The Film Festival

Film buffs will necessarily gravitate towards the Palais des Festivals beside the Vieux Port where Barry Norman and count-less other broadcasters report on the glitterati every May (it is perhaps not surprising that Cannes has now been officially twinned with Beverly Hills). And for fans an increasing number of the surrounding paving stones have been replaced with palm-prints of the stars, Hollywood-style (even directors like Polanski and Zefirelli have bent their backs over the wet cement).

Shopping

There are plenty of opportunities for shopping in the Rue d'Antibes and elsewhere and a particular speciality seems to be high-class prepared foods, with a number of *traiteurs* (a sort of delicatessen) competing vigorously to attract the discerning eye of finely coiffured ageing Frenchwomen. However, sensitive animal-loving types should pass quickly by the meat shops as the sight of tiny oven-ready birds, grisly skinned heads and unimaginable kinds of intestine can easily spoil the appetite.

Accommodation and Restaurants

As well as the famous 'Belle Epoque' palaces such as the Carlton (tel 93 68 91 68) and the Majestic (tel 93 68 91 00), sporting well over 200 rooms each, Cannes boasts nearly 130 other hotels (11 4-star, 32 3-star), 4800 rooms and more than 3000 apartments to let. Restaurants range from world class to the most humble, and *grand chefs* ply their trade at the Royal Gray, the Martinez (tel 93 94 30 30) and the Carlton.

Sports and Recreation

From pedaloes and jazz-dancing to waterskiing, and from tandem-surfboarding (two-man) and pony-trekking to the unimaginable *hydro-thalassothérapie,* Cannes is fully prepared for most requests in this field. Details available from the SI.

Excursions from Cannes

Whatever Cannes may have lost of its old charm and earlier elegance, it still has its share of the hinterland, which has not yet been irretrievably spoilt. There are enjoyable trips to be made to Super-Cannes and the Observatory of La Californie above the town; to Le Pézou, from which the view over the Gulf of La Napoule, the Esterel, Grasse and the foothills of the Alps is magnificent; and, from the old town in the west, to the Croix des Gardes, at the top of a 164 m (538 ft) hill. Further out there is Vallauris, with its potteries, and Golfe Juan; Antibes and the Plateau de la Garoupe on the Cape; and the Massif de l'Esterel, Mandelieu and Lougins. And among the most attractive sea-trips is one to the offshore Lérins Islands, St Honorat and Ste Marguerite.

The Lérins Islands

From the old harbour in Cannes two massive (24 m/79 ft) twin-hulled *Nautilus* ferries depart regularly to the Lérins Islands, carrying 100 passengers each. These unique catamarans have transparent floats and powerful underwater searchlights which produce spectacular views of the seabed both day and night (unfortunately one of the boats had sunk in the harbour when visited in l989). Typical fares are adults 60F, children 30F 10.30–21.30 (more expensive at night). There are also other smaller boats serving the route to the islands, but do not be surprised if the not-always-docile Mediterranean gives you a sharp shake-up on the way – it will make the pleasure of sailing into the lovely calm plateau between the islands all the more enjoyable.

Ste Marguerite, the larger and higher of the two islands, is not much more than a kilometre offshore. It is a pleasant, wooded spot, with a fortified château from the terrace of which there are fine views. (The Man in the Iron Mask was incarcerated here in 1687 and transferred to the Bastille in 1698.) St Honorat, separated from Ste Marguerite by the narrow, placid channel known as the Plateau du Milieu, looks more forbidding but is also beautifully wooded and well worth a visit. The island was famed in bygone days for its monastery, rebuilt in the 19th century, which produced no less than 20 saints, including St Patrick, and 600 bishops. The monastery, situated on a promontory, is visible from a considerable distance.

The islands are exceptionally rich in folklore, both religious and pagan. One of the most charming tales is that Ste Marguerite (according to local legend the sister of St Honorat) was so fond of her brother that she could not bear the separation enforced by the fact that men were not allowed to set foot on her island, and women were banned from his. St Honorat, touched by this devotion, nevertheless remained firm except for one concession: he would see his sister once a year, when the cherry trees were in bloom. Ste Marguerite prayed so long and so devoutly for an extension of this privilege that eventually one cherry tree in the island was allowed to blossom every month.

East of St Honorat the tiny Ilot de St Ferréol contained for a time the tomb of Paganini, who died of cholera in Nice in 1840. In 1845 his remains were transferred to Genoa.

Vallauris-Golfe Juan

The old town of Vallauris lies 2 km (1½ miles) inland from the popular seaside resort of Golfe-Juan where Napoleon stepped ashore in March 1815 after his escape from Elba (a plaque marks the spot – there is also a commemorative column). This is the start of the famous Route Napoleon. Together the two towns have a population of over 21,000 with SIs at 84 Ave de la Liberté,

Golfe-Juan (tel 93 63 73 12) and in the Square du 8 Mai 1945, Vallauris (tel 93 63 82 58). Golfe-Juan is also on the main SNCF coastal rail link.

Picasso at Vallauris
Apart from the Napoleon monuments, the main tourist sights are in Vallauris which has a castle (formerly a Lérins priory) which contains two museums and a chapel decorated by Picasso who had a studio here from 1947. When the artist was created an honorary citizen he presented Vallauris with a bronze statue of a man holding a sheep which now stands in the Place du Marche. The town also has an international reputation for its ceramics and there is a Pottery Museum (open daily 09.00–19.00) in the Rue Sicard. A Motor Museum is situated to the north of the town off the D135.

Accommodation and Restaurants
Vallauris has six modest (1-star) hotels whilst Golfe-Juan is somewhat better equipped with 15 listed by the SI, headed by the 3-star Hôtel les Jasmin (tel 93 63 80 83) on the N7, Le Petit Trianon (tel 93 63 70 51) at 18 Ave de la Liberté and Hôtel du Golfe (tel 93 63 71 22) at 81 Bvd des Frères Roustand. (For others and a list of furnished lettings see SI). There are also 20 restaurants in Vallauris and 28 in Golfe-Juan.

Sports and Recreation
A long stretch of sandy beach as well as a sizable yachting harbour and a wide range of sports make Golfe-Juan an attractive summer resort, and there are plenty of walks around Vallauris.

Grasse

Grasse, 18 km (11 miles) north of Cannes at the junction of the N85 with the N562 and N567, stands on the southern slopes of Roquevignon, which shelters it from the north. At an altitude ranging between 206 m (676 ft) and 526 m (1725 ft), it has a population of over 40,000, and a 3-star Syndicat d'Initiative (tel 93 36 03 56) at 3 Place de la Foux.

If you're not driving, the least stressful way of arriving (there is no train) is by bus from Cannes (15.60F from outside the SNCF station) or Nice (29F), but be sure to check return times from Grasse as the last buses tend to leave in mid-afternoon. With the windows open you can smell the perfumeries some distance away, which can eventually become oppressive, as Stendhal found in 1838: 'In my room I am haunted by a certain smell of resin which gives me a headache. It could well be the scent from the Grasse perfumery.'

The Old Town
In the Middle Ages, Grasse was a republic administered by a council of 'consuls' on the Italian model, and it remained in close relationship with Pisa until the Comte de Provence, Raymond-Berenger, terminated this arrangement, as well as Grasse's independent existence, in 1227.

The picturesque old town is delightful, with its basically 12th-century cathedral and watch-tower, and the Hôpital du Petit-Paris, the chapel of which possesses some fine paintings. There is also a Musée d'Art Provençal, a marine museum and a museum of miniature trains (opposite Parfumerie Gallimard on N85; open daily 09.00–20.00).

Jean-Honoré Fragonard
The French painter, Jean-Honoré Fragonard (1732–1806) was born in Grasse, the son of a tanner-glovemaker who had hoped that Jean-Honoré, having failed to become a competent craftsman, might become a clerk. Fragonard's father, incidentally, was a true representative of the older Grasse, in which tanning, soap-making and weaving were the major industries. The Villa Fragonard Museum (not to be confused with the Parfumerie Fragonard) has a good selection of the artist's work.

Apart from Fragonard, Grasse's most famous son was François de Grasse, Admiral of France (1723–88), who opposed the English during the American War of Independence. Visitors who made Grasse fashionable as a health resort include Pauline Borghese (Napoleon I's sister) and, later, Queen Victoria, who spent several winters here.

Perfume Capital of the World
Scent-making began in the 16th century when a Florentine settled in Grasse and saw the possibilities of exploiting the rosemary and lavender from the mountains. By the 18th century the master-perfumers were already a powerful group. In the 19th century flower-cultivation and scent-making entirely supplanted the older occupations to make Grasse, in its proud boast, 'the perfume capital of the world' (as featured in Patrick Süsskind's recent blockbuster *Das Parfum*). However, these days the hillsides are sadly depleted of the blooms that must have delighted the visitor in days of yore as it is now more economic to import flowers from North Africa. (Though roses for Chanel are grown at nearby

Pergomas.) All the perfume factories offer free guided tours and have adjoining shops selling Molinard, Gallimard and Fragonard products at prices to suit most pockets. There is also a recently opened international museum of *parfumerie*.

Accommodation and Restaurants

Grasse has one 4-star hotel, Le Regent (tel 93 36 40 10) on Route de Nice, and a 3-star hotel, Des Parfums (tel 93 36 10 10) at 1 Terrasses Tressemannes, but 16 others are listed in the SI's handbook as well as a number in the surrounding hill-villages. And there are 37 restaurants, many of which serve *cuisine grassoise*, particularly the stuffed-cabbage dish known as *lou fassum*, made in a specially designed string-bag called a *fassumier* (recipe in SI booklet). And if you've been wondering what the garishly coloured drinks are that other people always seem to be drinking, ask for *syrop à l'eau* (about 6F for a long glassful) in mint, blackcurrant etc flavours and get a cold, sticky disappointment.

Excursions from Grasse

Napoleon himself passed through Grasse on his return from Elba, as the Route Napoleon up from Cannes bears witness, and indeed this is a good way to explore the hinterland to the north. The surroundings of Grasse are particularly pleasant, including as they do the Gorges of the Loup and a wealth of excursions to such mountain villages as Gréolières, Gourdon and Cabris. Other places of interest are the Grotto of St Cezaire and, only 37 km (23 miles) north of Grasse, the winter-sports resort of Thorenc. (Immediately north of Thorenc lies the lovely mountain region of St André-les-Alpes, Castellane, Annot and Entrevaux.)

Antibes

Antibes, or Antibes-Juan-les-Pins, to give the joint communes their full title, has a permanent population of something like 40,000 inhabitants, but in the summer season visitors swell this number enormously, particularly in Juan. But although they now form one municipality, each fully justifies separate consideration.

Antibes is, like Menton, among the elite of the older attractions of the South of France in that these two, and few other places, have best survived the onslaught of mass tourism. What has to some extent saved it is its position tucked away on the eastern side of the rocky peninsula which is Cap d'Antibes. This means that, like other favoured capes in the Mediterranean, the main motor routes that scar the coast from end to end shoot across the neck of the peninsula, so that you have the twofold advantage of relative ease of access and a comforting detachment from the main stream of traffic.

Antibes makes the best of both worlds – the old and the new. There is still a pleasant combination of normal, busy, day-to-day life in an ancient centre of civilization and the thriving activity of a contemporary small port. Small wonder that so many artists and writers (Graham Greene has lived here for many years) are drawn to the place.

If you arrive by train at Antibes' flower-decked station, turn right at the exit and follow the Ave Robert Soleau into the central square, Place Général de Gaulle, where you will find the small and very crowded SI (tel 93 33 95 64). As well as an Antibes/Juan-les-Pins streetplan a useful leaflet to pick up is *A la Découverte du Vieil Antibes,* which gives a quided tour (French/English/German) of the old town.

Antibes belongs not only to tourism but to history. Founded on the site of a Ligurian camp during the 5th century BC by the Greeks (Phocoeans) – who were already established in Massilia (Marseilles) – the town was part of a chain of trading-posts, and was originally called Antipolis. (Indeed, history-proud residents still like to call themselves *Antipolitains* as an alternative to *Antibois.*) However, the Greek colonists had problems with the Ligurian tribes, and the Romans stepped in during the 2nd century AD, eventually taking over the whole area. Antibes, like Marseilles, held out for a long time but in the end a Roman fortified settlement rose on the site of the Greek acropolis, where the Château Grimaldi now stands.

Successive invasions and battles wrought havoc and in the 19th century a new town was built to the west of the old one, with its centre in what is now the Place de Gaulle.

Old Antibes
Enough remains of the old town to make it one of the most fascinating places of the whole coast. The ramparts have been largely retained, with houses built into them, and the one-way street which winds between the ramparts and the sea is one of old Antibes's main attractions. Narrow alleys and stairways under arches lead from the seaward road through the precincts of the château and the cathedral to the market and the ancient streets that plunge down through what remains of the old town towards the modern centre. It is a complex of endless interest.

The *Antibois* of the new town and the *Antipolitains* of the old are equally proud of the care with which the houses clustered within the ramparts have been restored and preserved. And there is, among the Graeco-Roman remains of Antipolis preserved in the archaeological section of the museum, what must be one of the ancient world's most touching relics – a tablet in memory of a 12-year-old boy. This youth came to the city with a company of actors and dancers towards the end of the 2nd century AD, danced for two days to the delight of his audience, and died. Neither the exact date nor the cause of death is stated, but seven palm-leaves in bas-relief symbolize the seven stars by which navigators find the North Star and thereby the dancer's name: Septentrion.

The old Port Vauban is also attractive and a high-level walkway around the harbour and château gives a good panoramic view of the coastline.

Museums
Apart from the remarkable Picasso Museum in the château which contains tapestries and ceramics as well as paintings, there is a museum of history and archaeology (Bastion St André), a regional history museum (Cours Massena) and, in the Ave Kennedy at Cap d'Antibes, the Musée Naval et Napoléonien. In addition, over 200 examples of the work of cartoonist/illustrator/sculptor Raymond Peynet are exhibited at the Musée Peynet (Place Nationale).

Antibes also hosts a number of festivals and international tournaments (bridge in May, jazz in July, for example) – details from the SI. And if you prefer familiar-looking banks, there is a Barclays and an American Express on Bvd Albert.

Accommodation and Restaurants
Antibes itself is less blessed with top-notch hotels than Juan-les-Pins, though there are eight 3-star establishments listed in the SI's brochure. However, Cap d'Antibes has the 4-star plus Cap Eden Roc (tel 93 61 39 01) on Bvd Kennedy and a large number of furnished apartments are available, as well as 10 campsites in the surrounding area. There are currently 61 restaurants listed, ranging in price from a modest 40F to 700F at Le Bacon (tel 93 61 50 02), Bvd de Bacon (the SI leaflet also gives details of house specialities). And if you're tiring of *croque monsieur* (ham and cheese on toast) and rolls in the snack line, one of a variety of filled *fougasses* (eg *fougasse jambon*, about 10F) makes a pleasant change.

Côte D'Azur

Sports and Recreation
The main beach in Antibes itself is the small sandy Plage de la Gravette by the old port but there are a number of others (Salis, La Garoupe etc) towards the Cape before the long stretches of Juan-les-Pins. Details of the usual aquatic sports can be obtained from the SI but, in addition, 3 km (2 miles) out of town on the N7 there is Marineland (performing dolphins, seals etc as well as a sea-elephant '*4 tonnes de tendresse*'!), the Aquasplash fun park and La Jungle de Papillons where you can wander through 900 sq. m (1076 sq. yd) of tropical gardens amongst 50 species of butterflies.

Juan-les-Pins

A short walk from Antibes down the Rue President Wilson brings you to the surprisingly dull-looking resort of Juan-les-Pins. The tourist office is at 51 Bvd Guillaumont on the seafront and if you haven't come to sun yourself or dance the night away (or spend all your life's savings at the Eden Beach Casino) your best bet is to head for the Jardin de la Pinede and sit quietly under the huge pine trees. If you are hungry there is certainly a wealth of eating establishments, indeed it almost seems that every street near the front is completely filled with seats at certain times of day (presumably the jet-setters stocking up for the frenetic activity after nightfall), and the hotels here are amongst the best on the Côte d'Azur, with three in the super-luxury 4-star L category – Belles Rives (tel 93 61 02 79), Helios (tel 93 61 55 25) and Juana (tel 93 61 08 70) – two 4-star, and 10 3-star.

Excursions from Antibes/Juan-les-Pins
From Antibes to Nice there are about 20 km (12 miles) of one of the dreariest coast roads in France, unredeemed even by the dramatic, if inappropriate, concrete ziggurats and pyramids which have sprung up in recent years on the edge of the sea. It is a fast road on which the driver is the most fortunate occupant of any car, in that he is obliged to keep his attention on the rest of the traffic until it is time to turn off for Nice Airport or inland to find an oasis in the concrete.

The coastline here combines the worst kind of ribbon development, with long stretches of nothingness between the road and the sea – beaches which appear to be without a local habitation or a name, wastelands not of nature but of man. These empty quarters are relieved – if that is the word – here and there by karting tracks and other diversions which look as though they have been dumped haphazardly between the road and the beach.

For the rest there are motels, garish shopping centres, play-grounds, Chinese junks, every kind of mechanical amusement it is possible for man in his desperation to devise. It must be one of the world's most appalling monuments to the failure of imagina-tion, environmental responsibility, intelligent planning and con-trol, preferable only to the much more harmful pollution of the sea. For if this stretch of road has been reduced to a meaningless track between two points, there is at least the sea on one side and a still-marvellous hinterland on the other. It may be easier one day to repair the harm done here than ever it will be to cleanse the worst stretches of the Mediterranean.

From Antibes, however, there are pleasant trips west and then north, by the D35 and the N85 to Mougins and Grasse.

Biot

Due north from Antibes, along the byways from the coast road, it is a comparatively short run to Biot (N7 and D4, 8 km/5 miles). Biot, which has become something of a shrine for admirers of the work of Fernand Léger, the French painter and ceramics artist, still retains much of its village quality. Perched on a low hill with fewer than 3000 inhabitants, it has a charming arcaded *place*, with a 15th-century church, and is an important centre for the production of grapes for the table, as well as flowers for the perfume industry at Grasse. There are three hotels, headed by the 3-star Hostellerie du Bois Fleuri (tel 93 65 68 74).

Villeneuve-Loubet

About 10 km (6 miles) along the coast road from Antibes to Nice, a left turn into the N85 can be the beginning of many other pleasant excursions. If you keep to the N85 you come almost immediately to Villeneuve-Loubet, a pleasant hill-town of nearly 4000 people, with a Syndicat d'Initiative at the Mairie, 16 hotels – including a number of well-recommended motels such as the Motel la Pétanque (tel 93 20 07 05) – and the Musée August Escoffier, a museum of culinary art. The town is only about 2 km (1½ miles) from Cagnes and 3 km (2 miles) from the coast, and also contains a house which was once the property of Marshal Pétain and is now a children's home.

Alternatively, soon after turning into the N85, the D36 forks left to Cagnes, St Paul-de-Vence, Vence and, by various delectable digressions, to Tourette-sur-Loup, Coursegoules, St Jeannet and many other pleasant spots. Another attractive route to Tourette-sur-Loup and to a whole chain of mountain villages begins at Villeneuve-Loubet, where the D7A, a right turn off the N85, leads into the N7 and opens up a fascinating area to explore.

Cagnes

Cagnes is still a typical Provençal hill-village, with old houses built into its ramparts. Between them, Haut-de-Cagnes (the hill-village), Cagnes Ville and Cros-de-Cagnes (the little port with a beach) have over 35,000 inhabitants and a 2-star Syndicat d'Initiative (tel 93 20 61 64) at 6 Bvd Maréchal Juin. The old village has a Renoir museum in the painter's former house, and many art galleries and exhibitions. There are about 25 hotels (including five in the 3-star category), mostly in Le Cros, and many camping and caravan sites in the area. A little road train runs from the Place de Gaulle to Haut-de-Cagnes (Apr–Oct, adults 25F, children 15F, duration 55 min), and also passes the great horse-racing arena known as the Hippodrome de la Côte d'Azur.

St Paul-de-Vence

St Paul-de-Vence, with a population of 2500, is a particularly attractive old hill-village, with the additional distinction that it also has the Fondation Maeght, which is claimed to be the most modern art gallery and art centre in Europe. Beautifully situated on the hill known as the Colline de St Paul, with terraced gardens, superb views, and sculpture effectively placed in the grounds, it consists of a number of well-designed buildings planned and designed by the architect José Luis Sert and decorated by some of the greatest artists of our time. It is intended to be an artistic and cultural meeting-place as well as an art gallery, and concerts and ballets are held here.

St Paul also has a picturesque Provençal fountain, medieval ramparts, a charming Provençal museum consisting of a replica of a 19th-century peasant's house, and an interesting collection of modern paintings in the Colombe d'Or. The SI is in the Maison de la Tour, Rue Grande. Of St Paul's eight hotels, six are 3-star and one, Mas d'Artigny (tel 93 32 84 54) in the Chemin des Salettes, is 4-star.

Vence

Near St Paul-de-Vence is Vence itself, a delightful hill-town sheltered from the north winds by the great limestone walls of the Baous (the Provençal name for rocky peaks), such as the Baou des

Blancs (673 m/2207 ft), the Baou St Jeannet (over 400 m/1312 ft) and the Puy de Tourettes (well over 1000 m/3280 ft). The promontory on which the town stands is more than 350 m (1148 ft) high and the light has an almost Greek quality. The purity of its famous spring of La Foux is known throughout the South, and the views from its old streets and archways would in themselves make a visit worth while. With just over 13,000 inhabitants and a 2-star SI in the Place du Grand Jardin, Vence offers a great deal to holidaymakers and to its fortunate permanent residents.

The 11th-century cathedral has Roman fragments built into the walls. There are five gates to the town, of which the most interesting is the Peyra Gate, through which one walks to the Place Peyra with its lovely Peyra Fountain and 15th-century tower. Outside the town there are many pleasant walks and drives (the SI produces a special handbook on these), among which a visit to the Chapelle du Rosaire, on the St Jeannet road (called Avenue Henri-Matisse), should not be missed.

La Chapelle du Rosaire
This is the chapel designed and decorated for the Dominican Sisters of Monteils (Aveyron) by the French painter Matisse, who died in Nice in l954, aged 84. Walls, floor and ceiling are of white marble, and the altar is of the warm-coloured stone from Rogny which the Romans used to build the Pont du Gard. The stained-glass windows are in luminous tints of lime yellow, the green of fresh young shoots, and a pure Mediterranean blue. Matisse's line-drawings on white tiles echo the black-and-white of Dominican garments, but in daylight they are bathed in a brilliant, almost unearthly radiance from the windows. The artist himself said that what he had attempted to do was to take a confined space and, by the interplay of colour and line, create the impression of infinity. The chapel is open to the public on Tuesdays and Thursdays unless religious festivals fall on those days. Work began on the chapel in 1947, when Matisse was 77, and the completed building was consecrated on 25 June 1951, three years before the artist's death.

Accommodation
Vence has two 4-star hotels, one of which, the Château St Martin (tel 93 58 02 02) on the Route de Coursegoules is in the luxury class, and 12 other more modest establishments.

Excursions from Vence
A pleasant 17 km (10 miles) run from Vence by the D2 takes you over the Col de Vence to Coursegoules, a tiny village of sheep-

farmers at about 1000 m (3280 ft), with the backcloth of the Cheiron (about 1900 m/6232 ft).

Within easy reach are the pleasant Tourette-sur-Loup to the west, La Gaude, Gattières, Carros and many other excellent *points-de-repère* to the north, with the winter resorts of Valberg and Auron still further north. If you propose to explore the Vence area in detail the French Carte de France, 1/50,000, Type 1922, Feuilles XXXVI 42-43-44 and adjoining sections is recommended.

One of the impressive, if not exactly picturesque, views you get from La Gaude is the industrial zone of Nice along the bank of the River Var below you. It appears to be an imaginative development which attracts workers from many of the villages where scenic beauty and the tourist trade are not really enough to stimulate and feed the out-going younger generation. Local workers have the choice of living in the industrial zone or commuting from their hill-villages, which will thus, it is hoped, not be entirely abandoned to the elderly and the holidaymakers.

St Jeannet

East and north-east of Vence, in the upper reaches of the River Cagne, there are many attractive routes and places. St Jeannet, at the foot of the Baou de St Jeannet, is quiet and restful, with magnificent views. Although table grapes have largely taken the place of wine production, there is still available (if you ask in the right places) a white wine of St Jeannet which has something of the radiance and clarity of the Matisse chapel. There are two 1-star hotels, the Auberge Saint-Jeannet (tel 93 24 90 06) and the Sainte-Barbe Grill (tel 93 24 94 38), both in the Place Ste Barbe.

Below St Jeannet, in the Vallon de la Cagne, where the stripling river tumbles fresh and sparkling over rocks and rapids in friendly ravines, there are a number of ancient mills. If country quiet in the mountains, with a stream at your door and fireflies to light your evening stroll, appeals to you, seek out this corner of France. A tough little car is desirable but not entirely indispensable. There are tracks where a mule would be more useful. If you stay long enough you will find that you can, in fact, walk everywhere you want to go and there are buses from Vence or St Jeannet.

St Laurent du Var

Nestling on the banks of the River Var, between Nice and Cagnes, St Laurent's history goes back to the Bronze Age, and the fast-flowing waters of its river have been an obstacle for both pilgrims and invaders alike over the years. By the 11th century, Castrum Agrimantis, the old town, had been established on the fertile banks of the Var but was all but wiped out by the plague and laid to waste. However, it was later rebuilt and in the 19th century a bridge was built over the river, the centre of which marked the boundary between France and the Kingdom of Sardinia. St Laurent now has a population of over 26,000 and is easily reached by road and rail. The SI (tel 93 07 87 01) is situated at 136 Bvd Point du Jour.

The old town can be found upstream of the two modern bridges and has a 15th-century church and the remains of an 11th-century monastery, and there are pleasant walks to be had in the flower-growing areas in the hills of the Montaleigne district to the north. The modern part of the town, however, is mostly devoted to sports and leisure, though they are proud to have been awarded a prize in the annual Floral Towns competition in 1988 and won the Blue Flag for clean beaches the same year.

Accommodation and Restaurants
The hotels are headed by the 4-star Héliôtel Marine (tel 93 31 51 51) in Ave St Hubert but there are also three 3-star establishments amongst others, a wide range of furnished apartments to let and two campsites. The SI's handbook lists 11 restaurants and says that if you want to eat in the Yacht Harbour there are 4000 seats to choose from!

Sports and Recreation
The main feature of St Laurent is its huge Yacht Harbour which, with 1063 berths, is one of the largest on the Riviera. There are also swimming-pools and all kinds of sports from volley-ball to *hobie-cat* (details from the SI).

Nice

The Var, once described as 'before 1860 a line of demarcation between the easy-going semi-Italian people to the east and the more energetic French population to the west...', brings us to Nice, capital of the Côte d'Azur and, with a population of more than 400,000, one of France's great cities.

The differences in character between Nice and Cannes are too complex to be gone into here, but almost everybody who knows this coast well has a marked preference for one or the other. Rarely do you find the anti-crowds, anti-big-city visitor who

Côte D'Azur

dislikes them both. Most often, in my experience, the visitor, offered a theoretical choice spending some time in either city, will say, 'After all, there is something rather special about Nice...'

Nice is not only the 4-star plus Negresco and almost 300 other officially listed hotels, it is also the Babazouk – the old town and port. It is not only elaborate carnivals and flower festivals, but also a unviersity city of growing academic and general cultural importance. It is not only the spacious Place Masséna, but also the Cours Saleya and the flower market.

If travelling by train without booking ahead, turn left out of the station for the Accueil de France branch of the SI (tel 93 87 07 07) in Ave Thiers. (The main tourist office is at 5 Ave Gustave V near the seafront at Ruhl Plage (tel 93 87 60 60).) Don't be put off by the crowds of backpackers as there seem to be plenty of rooms, from 1- to 4-star, after 10.00. Join a queue and be patient. (This remarkable service also allows you to book rooms anywhere in France that is a member of 'Accueil de France'.) Alternatively, dump your gear in one of the electronic *consignes* (12F upwards, and the only way to get change is to buy sweets etc in one of the kiosks) and head for the beach.

Nice is extremely well served for transport, as befits the fifth-largest city in France. There is a direct TGV link to Paris (7 hours, 3 trains a day June–September), many intercity trains and buses stop here, and an international airport is situated 5 km (3 miles) to the west of the city centre.

Ancient Nike

Historically, Nice is of great interest. Founded in 350BC by the Greeks of Marseilles, it began originally as a small trading post. The site of the original settlement was on the Rocher du Château (Castle Rock) and on the left bank of the mouth of the Paillon – the river which forms the dividing line between the old and new towns today (now partly covered in and built over). Prehistoric remains have been found in the caves of the rock. There seems no doubt that there was also a Ligurian camp on the hill of Cimiez, but the city proper really began with the Greek market settlement on the rock, which was given the proud name of Nike (Victory). The Romans later preferred the Cimiez site, but both centres were destroyed in the barbarian invasions. An unimportant little town-ship, which was all that was left of Nice, then passed from the power of one lordling to another until 1388, when it came under the Duke of Savoy's protection.

In the 17th and 18th centuries Nice was bandied back and forth between France and Italy until the unification of Italy followed an alliance between Napoleon III and Victor-Emmanuel of Savoy Piedmont in 1859, when Nice and Savoy were returned to France. Older members of the present generation will remember Mussolini's abortive battle-cry – 'Nice, Tunis, Corsica!'

Two of Nice's famous sons are the great General Masséna and Giuseppe Garibaldi. Smollett spent some time here recovering from TB and Matisse lived here from 1917 until his death in l954.

Museums
Nice is a marvellous city of museums and galleries. Furniture, paintings and Provençal pottery are in the Musée Masséna, there is a fine art collection in the Musée Cheret (or Musée des Beaux Arts), another museum is devoted to Matisse in Cimiez, where he had his studio (reopening 1990), and there is a Chagall Museum nearby. There are museums of Old Nice, natural history, and the fascinating Palais des Lascaris in the Rue Droite.

The Old Town
The old town is delightful, either during the day when the main courtyard, Cours Saleya, is filled with market stalls or in the evening under a dramatically red sky when some of the finest-looking *plats* of the Riviera are served up to Nice's smarter set (cheaper eating can be had in the shadow of the cathedral in Place Rossetti a few blocks to the north, and there are some excellent Italian restaurants tucked away in back alleys). Particularly recommended is a visit to the Tour Ballanda (with its free naval museum) and the site of the former château for spectacular views of the city – this is the view of the Promenade des Anglais you see in the postcards, complete with strange succulents with flowers like upside-down yellow hairbrushes. There is a lift if the steps look offputting, but you will miss the intermediate vistas and the waterfall.

Whilst in the vicinity, there is a human sundial (laid out 21 June 1981) at Pte des Ponchettes with calibrations for your own shadow from 07.00 to 18.00, and round the promontory in the direction of Villefranche is a gigantic war memorial hewn out of the rockface that is floodlit at night (architect Roger Seassal, sculptor Alfred Janniot).

Other sights include the Palais de Justice, the fountains and strange C-shaped sculpture in Espace Masséna/Jardin Albert 1er, the opera house and the new Acropolis complex behind the

Côte D'Azur

Esplanade Kennedy (full list of 17 free museums and galleries from SI). And an often forgotten gem in the bleak streets to the west of the station, the beautiful Russian Orthodox Cathedral in Ave Nicolas, with its sadly neglected gardens.

Another recent addition (open March 1989) is the 6-acre (3-hectare) Parc des Miniatures which traces Nice's history in 1/25th-scale replicas of its buildings etc (Bvd Imperatrice Eugenie in the Fabron district, about 3 km (2 miles) west of the centre off the Autoroute Urbane Sud). Nice also hosts many international festivals and concerts (see SI for details) including the spectacular Battle of the Flowers (20-odd flower-bedecked floats cruise down the Promenade des Anglais) and a famous carnival dating from 1878.

Cimiez
Cimiez, the health resort of Nice on the top of a hill to the north of the city, still bears the cachet of Queen Victoria's approval and is still inclined to think of itself as the aristocratic quarter. The huge hotel at the top of Bvd Cimiez, with its statue of Victoria in front, is indeed impressive and many of the streets in the surrounding area (all filled with palatial residences) are named after British royalty. Cimiez has the remains of a Roman amphitheatre which held 6000 spectators; a Villa des Arènes which contains not only the archaeological museum but also the Musée Matisse already mentioned; a rather scruffy public park; and a beautifully tended monastery garden, from which there are good views of Nice. Two other eminences close to Nice which make pleasant short trips are Mont Alban (about 240 m/787 ft) and Mont Boron (about 170 m/ 558 ft). These hills mark the eastern frontier of Nice, between the Paillon Valley and the port of Villefranche.

Accommodation and Restaurants
There are hundreds of hotels and apartments to let in Nice, from the magnificent Negresco (tel 93 88 39 51) at 37 Promenade des Anglais downwards. And a 32-page booklet from the SI lists every variety of restaurant with its particular specialities etc, even down to what credit cards they take and whether they allow dogs or have facilities for the handicapped. Traditional dishes to try are *salade niçoise*, *pissaladière* (Nice's own variety of pizza) and, if you've not already tried it elsewhere in Provence, *soupe de poissons* (thick fish soup served with chunky croutons, grated cheese and *rouille*).

Sports and Recreation
Nice offers 30 beaches (15 public, 15 private) spread over 3½ km

(2 miles) and there is plenty of room for all. Indeed, here it almost seems *de rigueur* to be carrying either a baguette or a rolled beachmat under one's arm. Be warned, however, when you plunge into the sea having carefully noted which sunshade you left your towel by – like as not the parasol will have departed with its owner by the time you return. Whether you like parachuting over the waves whilst being towed by a speedboat, playing with the high-rollers in the casinos (2), or ice-skating, there is something for everyone (there is even a Scrabble club). Nearby Cagnes-sur-Mer also has a huge horse-racing track (*hippodrome*), and an amusement park, Zygofolis, is situated to the north-west of the city off the A8 at St Isidore.

The Nice Region

Well worth a visit is the hinterland of this last stretch of the Côte d'Azur, the area known as the Nice region. This may be roughly defined as the area limited to the west by a line from Nice to the winter resort of Auron 97 km (60 miles) away, to the north by a line running east-west through St Etienne-de-Tinée, to the east by a line running from Menton through Sospel and the Vallée de la Vésubie to St Martin-Vésubie, and to the south by the Mediterranean.

The Nice region is still one of the best places in Europe for a summer holiday, with a more dependable proportion of sun than anywhere else – Cannes has an annual average of about 220 days of sunshine; in Menton it is estimated that there are rarely more than 30 really sunless days in the whole year. If some parts of the coast are crowded during the summer peak, the hinterland is rich in mountain villages and small towns where you can still bask in the afternoon sun in the quiet central *place*. Some of the villages are well known, but there are still many for the visitor to discover, a few kilometres either side of the secondary roads. The following suggestions are intended more to put you on the track of your own discoveries than to offer a set programme.

Almost due north from Nice, for example, driving inland for anything between 110 and 150 km (70 and 93 miles), depending on detours, there is the valley of the Var; the rocky cleft of the Mescla, 37 km (23 miles); the hill-village of Touet, 55 km (34 miles), with its church built over a mountain stream; Puget-Théniers, 64 km (40 miles); Entrevaux, 71 km (44 miles); the gorges of the Daluis (a diversion from the N202 along the D29); Guillaumes, 97 km (60 miles), with its fine road cut through the rock to the Var; and Valberg, 110 km (70 miles), a winter-sports centre as well as a summer resort. Beyond this point there is another winter-sports centre, Beuil, which is perched on a rock but surrounded by meadows, and the awe-inspiring gorges of the Cians.

A more ambitious run, which gives a comprehensive idea of the attractions of the hinterland, can be made from Nice to Menton by way of Peira Cava and Sospel (roughly 200 km, 124 miles). This would take you from Nice up the Paillon Valley (N204) to the vineyards and orchards of Contes, 18 km (11 miles); then on to L'Escarene and up to Lucéram (N566), 34 km (21 miles); to Peira Cava (D21), 48 km (30 miles); and back to Sospel (N566), 8l km (50 miles). Here you could make a rewarding diversion (D43) to Fontan, La Brigue and Tende. From Sospel to Menton the Col de Castillon (about 800 m/2624 ft) gives a view of the Carei River winding down to the sea at Menton.

This naturally suggests the riches of the immediate hinterland of Menton itself, with the lovely and still largely unspoilt hill-villages of Castellar, Gorbio, Ste Agnès and Castillon with their surrounding hills and lush valleys.

Variations on the theme of excursions through the hinterland between Nice and Menton are many and delightful. There are various ways from Cagnes to the Gorges of the Verdon. Worth exploring, for example, is the country round St Martin-Vésubie, the high-altitude resort in the Alpes-Maritimes at the foot of the group of mountains which rise to the Argentera (over 305 m/ 1000 ft). There is another winter-sports resort nearby at La Colmiane. Another particularly fine drive from Nice goes through the gorges of La Mescla (37 km/23 miles) by the N202 to La Tour, Clans and St Sauveur (N205), and on to St Etienne-de-Tinée (117 km/73 miles), in the upper valley of the Tinée, which is a summer resort and climbing centre. Then, 7 km (5 miles) further on, there is Auron, the most important winter-sports resort of the southern Alps. If you return to Nice by D39, N205 and N202 the round trip from Nice to Nice will amount to something under 250 km (156 miles).

Back to the coast of coasts, the incomparable Riviera Côte d'Azur. The way east can be taken by the magnificently scenic Grande Corniche (now the A8) which climbs through the foothills by way of La Turbie and Eze, or along the coast road (N7) to the Italian frontier.

Villefranche

If you leave Nice by the old port, driving round its northern end and along the Boulevard Carnot (N559), a 6 km (4 miles) run round the peninsula of Mont Boron brings you to Villefranche, sheltered between the headland of Nice and Cap Ferrat. Villefranche, with its SI in the Jardin François Binon, is still a picturesque fishing port, with a large tourist harbour and a sheltered roadstead deep enough not only for liners and ships on pleasure-cruises, but also for naval vessels – particularly, during the post-war years, United States warships.

With something over 7400 inhabitants and about a dozen good hotels, including five 3-star establishments, Villefranche is one of the most popular health and holiday resorts, and has a shingle beach. The 16th-century citadel and fortifications, and the old town, make a pleasant setting, and the poet-painter Jean Cocteau decorated the Chapelle St Pierre in the Port de la Sante. Where the Corniche Inferieure approaches Beaulieu across the neck of Cap Ferrat, the Avenue D. Semeria branches off to take you into the heart of the cape.

Cap Ferrat

Cap Ferrat has become best known as one of the favourite resorts of the royal, the rich and the famous. Leopold II of the Belgians bought the Villa Leopolda, and his son Albert I often stayed there. The villa was later sold to the owner of Fiat. The writer Somerset Maugham lived in the Villa Mauresque, where Winston Churchill was a frequent guest. Fortunately, however, the peninsula is not restricted to the royal, the rich and the renowned: like all the capes along this coast, it gains enormously from the fact that the main coast road goes straight across its neck, leaving the rest of the peninsula luckily deprived of the means of mass entertainment but generously endowed with natural beauty, quiet, and charm.

There are about a dozen hotels, two of them 4-star plus – the Grand (tel 93 76 00 21) and the Voile d'Or (tel 93 76 13 13) – a delightful museum (the Musée Ile-de-France) surrounded by beautiful gardens and built in 1914 by the Baroness Ephrussi de Rothschild on what she once described as 'the most beautiful spot in the world', and a zoo. The fishing and holiday village of St Jean-Cap-Ferrat has 2356 inhabitants (SI at 12 Avenue Claude Vigon), and there are both sandy and shingle beaches. A footpath round the cape gives good views of Beaulieu and Cap d'Ail.

Beaulieu

The Promenade Maurice Rouvier links St Jean with Beaulieu (1½km/1 mile), probably the most sheltered spot along the whole French Mediterranean coast during the winter. (It is one of the places where you will see not only lemon, orange and palm trees but also bananas, although the only fruit I have seen on the stems has looked more decorative than edible.)

Beaulieu, with a 2-star SI in the Place de la Gare, has a population of 4300, and of its score of hotels two are 4-star plus, including the world-famous Réserve de Beaulieu (tel 93 01 00 01) and the Métropole (tel 93 01 00 08). (The Carlton (tel 93 01 14 70) is also 4-star.) It is an elegant resort, with a delightful replica of a Greek villa, the Villa Kerylos.

Eze

From 'Little Africa' – the strip of coast between the rocky slopes and the sea where Beaulieu stands – the road brings us to Eze-sur-Mer, a resort with a shingle beach and a pleasant setting that has grown up at the foot of the old village of Eze (formerly a medieval fortress), perched on the 427 m (1400 ft) rocky eminence of Mont Bastide.

Eze has a population of 2500 and the SI is in the Mairie behind the station. The old village is one of the most picturesque and splendidly situated of all the hill-villages close to the coast. However, it is now in danger of being spoilt by tourism. Indeed, there is nothing so disappointing than to tramp for an hour up the sweltering rocky path from the little seaside resort to arrive amongst bustling hordes of fresh-faced visitors who have reached the village from the Corniche motor route behind. Antiques, bric-à-brac, and gifte shoppes seem to sprout from every nook and cranny of the narrow streets and even the admittedly magnificent view from the top isn't free as the remains of the old castle are surrounded by an exotic garden of cacti and succulents (admission 8F). One consolation, perhaps, is that Nietzsche once trod the same rocky path and thought out his masterpiece *Also Sprach Zarathrustra* along it.

In the Chapelle des Penitents Blancs there is a Christ in wood of the Spanish school (1258), of the type you would be more likely to find in Roussillon and the Pyrenees. Mounted over a skull and cross-bones it is known as the Christ of the Black Death and bears an inscription in Catalan which says: 'As you are now, so once was I, and as I am now so shall you be.' The chapel, not to be confused with the church, is not open to the public, though you may peer in through a grille covering the doorway. The church itself is filled with soft piped music and features a strange pulpit with a projecting human arm holding a black crucifix and, for some reason, a model sailing ship hangs from the ceiling.

Accommodation
For such a small town, Eze has some remarkably prestigious hotels with no less than three, including the Cap Estel (tel 93 01 50 44) on the seafront, in the 4-star category.

Cap d'Ail

4 km (3 miles) east of Eze is Cap d'Ail which, in its small, comparatively secluded and formerly somewhat exclusive way, has retained much of the natural cachet of the wooded capes along this coast. It is an excellent health and bathing resort, with fine beaches shaded by pines. There is much to see in the immediate neighbourhood and there are nine hotels and a number of camping sites, including the University City Club. From Cap d'Ail eastwards the road, dominated by the Tête de Chien, leads temporarily out of France into the Principality of Monaco (covered in the next chapter) and on to Menton.

Menton

Menton is still the queen of the Riviera. A modern queen, perhaps not terribly smart, even a little blowzy, but in complexion, health, confidence and natural superiority, a queen all the same. She was born to be queen: nowhere along the whole Mediterranean coastline of France, from Cerbère to Ventimiglia, are conditions more propitious for a royal birth and a regal life. Senseless, money-grubbing damage is being done all round her and many of her most charming attributes have already been reduced to memories, but while relics of the reign of Menton remain the Riviera will never be entirely lost.

Today Menton (with its modern suburb, Carnolès) has more than 30,000 inhabitants and a most efficient and obliging Syndicat d'Initiative (tel 93 57 57 00)) in the impressive Palais d'Europe, Avenue Boyer (pick up their indispensable 150-page booklet *Menton Roquebrune L.M. dans la Poche* for details of all the town's facilities). These figures are swollen considerably during the summer season, but not, perhaps, to the rather terrifying extent that prevails in some of the younger, trendier resorts.

Côte D'Azur

History
It is a long story. Local legend takes it back to Adam and Eve, for it
was Eve who, clutching a lemon to her breast as she and Adam
were driven from Eden, made no attempt to plant it until she
came to a spot between blue sea and great mountains where
conditions were ideal. This was Menton, where the golden fruit
flourishes in the gardens and at the sheltered feet of the Alps.

Fanciful legends apart, man discovered the advantages of living
here as long ago as the Palaeolithic and Neolithic eras, as the
skeletons of Grimaldi and Cro-Magnon men found in the Red
Rock caves on what is now the French-Italian frontier indicate.

These early settlers were followed by a great variety of visitors,
temporary and otherwise, ranging from Romans, Saracens, Ligurians and the Grimaldis of Monaco to Queen Victoria of Great
Britain, the Empress Elizabeth of Austria, the Empress Eugénie,
King Albert of the Belgians, sundry other royals and a liberal
sprinkling of statesmen, writers (including Katherine Mansfield
and Blasco Ibanez) and artists – all of whom have left their mark
and have contributed to the unique quality of this evergreen
family holiday resort.

The town grew on a gently sloping stretch of coast between the
promontory of Cap Martin and the cliffs of La Mortola, and is
sheltered by a ring of Alpine peaks ranging from Mont Agel (1097 m/
3598 ft) on the west to Mont Grammont (1378 m/4520 ft) on the
frontier with Italy. Thanks to this protective screen, which also
refreshes Menton with the four streams of the Gorbio, the
Borrigo, the Carei and the Fossan, the mistral is practically
unknown in this area, and the vegetation is unusually luxuriant.
Menton's value as a health resort is known throughout the world,
and though the old town and Garavan have suffered some
undesirable changes since the resort's Victorian heyday – beyond
the leisuredly Boulevard de Garavan there are now motorways
slicing through the mountains to the Italian frontier, with a flurry
of brash new hotels on the seafront and a huge new pleasure port
– enough remains of the old flavour to attract the discriminating
holidaymaker still.

Old Menton
What Menton still has to offer, above all, is a modern West End
with everything mass tourism needs and, in Old Menton itself,
one of the loveliest hill-towns of all, climbing through narrow
ways and by an elegant stone stairway to the Church of St Michel
and the Chapelle des Pénitents-Blancs – both classical 17th-

century buildings which partly enclose the *parvis* (square) where the annual chamber-music festival is held in August.

This is an enchanted setting. Two sides consist of the elegant façades of the two churches at right angles to each other, with the *parvis* of St Michel serving as the stage for the orchestra or soloist; the third side consists of the tall houses at the top of the old town, whose windows are filled with townspeople enjoying the concerts; and the fourth side is open to the Mediterranean – a fabulous backcloth to a unique setting. The only drawbacks are so rare as to be hardly worth considering: once in a while the acoustics fall below the level of an enclosed concert hall, and there are occasional intrusive sounds from the alleys of the old town surrounding the churches – village voices, unguarded footsteps, the occasional cat or dog...the normal sounds of living which enhance, rather than interrupt the music. As for the quality of the music (everything except the latest novelty), some of the participants over the past 15 years or so have included: Artur Rubinstein, Igor Oistrakh, Nathan Milstein, I Musici, Glenn Gould, Samson François, the Hungarian Quartet, the Stuttgart Chamber Orchestra, Wilhelm Kempf, the Vegh Quartet, Biron Janis, Jean-Pierre Rampal, I Virtuosi di Roma, Christian Ferras, Boris Christoff and many others. And since 1977, the violinist Ivry Gitlis has added his own music festival in the suburb of Garavan's lovely municipal olive-grove, Le Pian. Music in such a setting, in an ancient town of such charm, sums up the appeal of Menton.

Sightseeing
Within the complex of Carnolès-Menton-Garavan itself there is an abundance of entertainment and interest, cultural, sporting and traditional. On the one hand there is the municipal casino, gaming-rooms, swimming-pools and an elaborate promenade, and on the other the museum and library with its fascinating relics of Menton's long struggles for independence and its French-Italian history. The Hôtel de Ville also has its register office (or, more romantically, marriage chamber) decorated by Jean Cocteau and there is a Cocteau Museum in the Bastion of the port. Other sights include the 18th-century Palais Carnolès Museum (formerly the home of the Prince of Monaco), the Municipal Museum and Les Colombières – a fantastic Renaissance garden designed by the local poet Ferdinand Bac, with a first-class hotel and swimming-pool, marvellous walks amid classical statuary, and some of the finest views of the whole coast. Menton is particularly proud of its horticulture, having recently won the national Floral Town competition four years running. There is also a Lemon Festival in February.

Côte D'Azur

But the essence of Menton, like the essence of all the old Mediterranean French coastal settlements that survive with some of their character intact, is compounded of tree-lined small squares where shopkeepers, local residents, visitors, children, café waiters and the old villagers can rest in the sun or the shade; cool, narrow alleyways under frequent arches; miraculous markets which are a joy to explore and even greater pleasure to shop in; and ancient villas with paradisal gardens climing the slopes to the Boulevard de Garavan.

Accommodation

Those who have known Menton over the years will regret that the pleasant old Hôtel des Anglais is, alas, no more but there are still quite a few of the older establishments, such as the modest New York (2-star (tel 93 35 78 69)) situated on the Ave Katerine Mansfield. Apart from the 4-star Ambassadeurs (tel 93 57 52 52) at 2 Rue du Louvre there are 11 3-star hotels but dozens of smaller places (such as the 1-star Villa Louise (tel 93 35 72 39) at 10 Ave Katerine Mansfield) can be found in the quiet corners between the beach and the Boulevard de Garavan.

Excursions from Menton

Apart from the many advantages of Menton itself as a holiday centre its hinterland and surroundings are well worth exploring.

Immediately inland are the mountain villages of Castellar, St Agnès, Gorbio and many others, all accessible by car, local bus, or on foot. Each has its own character and charm, and each is a splendid centre for wanderings on foot through a lovely countryside. Take, for example, the track from Gorbio to Roquebrune. It is an easy, winding way, all on about the same contour line, so that when you reach the château of Roquebrune the simplest route is then down to the sea road to get the bus back to Menton. The café in the square at Gorbio, incidentally, has a terrace overlooking an extraordinarily lush wooded valley – something of an oasis among the less richly endowed slopes.

These are but a few of the local excursions: there are also delightful trips to be made to Cap Martin-Roquebrune, Monte Carlo and Monaco, the valleys of the Borrigo and the Castagnins, the Carei Valley and, more ambitiously but with abundant reward, as far as Castillon, Sospel, Tende and Brigue.

Royal Palace, Monaco

The Principality of Monaco

Basically Monaco is a 3½ km(2 mile)-long chunk of coastal mountainside at the extreme eastern end of the Côte d'Azur, which finally became independent from France in 1861, and whose tiny area is a legendary symbol of international high life. Despite this you can enter from France without a passport.

The principality is ruled over by Prince Rainier, who was born in 1923, acceded in 1949, married the famous American film star Grace Kelly in 1956 (she was tragically killed in a car crash in 1982) and operates more as the chief executive of a corporation than as a traditional monarch. His heir is Prince Albert and he has two sophisticated and headline-hitting daughters, the Princesses Caroline and Stephanie.

Monaco's 30,000 inhabitants not only enjoy one of the most

The Principality of Monaco

valuable pieces of real estate anywhere in the world, the 5500 of them who are true Monegasques pay no taxes. This privilege was ordained by the founding father of present-day Monaco, Charles III, who both abolished taxes in 1863 and exempted his native citizens from military service.

Geographically Monaco has three focal points: Monaco proper, known as the Rock, which is the capital; Monte Carlo on the other hill, housing the three Casinos and the best hotels and shops; and the Condamine, which is the sea-level section between the two. There is also the recently transformed industrial area of Font-veille, extending westwards from the Rock towards Cap d'Ail. The Tourist Office is on the Boulevard des Moulins (tel 93 30 87 01).

The Grimaldi Family
The principality has had an astonishing 1000-year-long linkage with its ruling Grimaldi family, although few decades of those centuries can have witnessed as much change and improvement as has been achieved since Prince Rainier succeeded his grand-father, Louis II, in 1949.

The name of Grimaldi first appears as that of a baron who fought well against the Saracen invaders in the 10th century, but it was not until the 13th century that the Grimaldis became firmly installed on the rock that is now Monaco. Some of them were allies of the kings of France, others acquired domains in Provence. The Grimaldi who won formal recognition of his extensive holdings was Charles I, Admiral of France, Baron of San Demetrio, Lord of Monaco, Rocquebrune, Menton and Ventimi-glia. He was, incidentally, wounded at the Battle of Crécy.

The Genoese, who had formerly held Monaco, tried to take it back from Charles I's successor, Rainier II, but were eventually forced to renounce their claim. Monaco then became independent under the protection of France and Piedmont-Savoy. Various changes of allegiance took place during the following centuries and after the French Revolution Monaco was temporarily attached to the Alpes-Maritimes Department of France. In 1861, following the Italian war of independence, Charles III struck a deal with France. He handed over Menton and Roquebrune in return for the withdrawal of French garrisons and a substantial payment. The boundaries established in 1861 remain today.

20th-Century Changes
Monte Carlo has, of course, been famous as a haunt of interna-tional society since Victorian times: as Charles III intended it to

be. But even by his standards the second half of the 20th century has seen a quite extraordinary reinforcement of the principality's fortunes, ranging from a hard-won agreement with France for a share in the VAT revenue of the Alpes-Maritime Department to an actual increase of 31 hectares (76 acres) in its exploitable area, largely through the reclamation of land from the sea with elaborate concrete polders and dykes. Such an acreage may not sound much until you realize that the entire extent of Monaco is only 156 hectares (386 acres), roughly equivalent in size to Hyde Park in London or one sixtieth of Paris.

Future Plans

Soon the development potential will be further enhanced by Prince Rainier's plans for the future. Back in 1964 the Paris to Ventimiglia railway was diverted into a 3 km (2 miles) tunnel under the Monte Carlo and adjacent Beausoleil hills, thus adding some 5 hectares (2 acres) to the available land as well as healing an ugly scar on the principality. Now its remaining overground track will be built on. More significantly, a giant sea-wall is to be thrown out across the entire waterfront to provide an anchorage for cruise ships in addition to the multi-million-dollar private yachts that crowd the existing harbour. At the same time the light-industrial area of Fontveille has been reconstructed to provide a marina, a heliport at the sea's edge, and what must be the most elegant football stadium anywhere. Rainier is indeed a prince among developers.

Today's visitors to this fairytale state who find themselves shocked by the skyscrapers and the development of the waterfront – regarded by some as a disfigurement of the site's natural beauty – can take comfort from the fact that it might have been much worse. The destruction of Monaco's scenic grandeur was halted, it is claimed, before it was too late. Prince Rainier's other proud boast is that his small but well-equipped police force has made Monaco the most secure and crime-free place on the Mediterranean coast.

The Rock – Monaco Town

Development or no development, Monaco retains a considerable variety of attractions. Among them are the Botanical Gardens, the Zoological Acclimatization Centre and the world-famous Oceanographic Museum, run under the direction of the renowned French underwater explorer, Jacques Cousteau. However, the operatic glamour of the stone-turreted Palace is probably the greatest draw to visitors.

The Principality of Monaco

The Palace
The Prince's Palace stands in a square that takes up the whole width of the Rock. Begun by the Genoese in 1215, it is a largely Renaissance structure, with gardens overlooking the sea. There are particularly fine views from the Promenade Ste Barbe adjoining it. Many parts of the Palace and its approaches can be visited during the season, except for the private gardens on the northwest side. A charge is made for addmission, although children under ten are let in free.

The Old Town
The old town and the Palace are now reached not only on foot up the old streets, but also by an amazing system of tunnels and underground facilities excavated from the Rock itself. These enable visitors to be deposited by coaches at the bottom and taken up concealed escalators into the heart of the old town, thus keeping the streets free of traffic. It is a neat arrangement, if more reminiscent of Disneyland than Mediterranean sophistication.

The Cathedral in the old town has a notable collection of primitive paintings. The Oceanographic Museum, with its aquarium, stands on the cliff edge and its terrace has excellent views, as do the nearby St Martin's gardens. The best-known restaurant is the Castelroc, on the Place du Palais (February to November), but it is closed in the evening: the Rock is not the place for nightlife.

The Condamine
The area lying along the waterfront between the Rock and Monte Carlo, La Condamine, is an interesting and indeed essential part of the Monaco complex. Not only does it shelter the Church of Ste Devote and the Zoological Centre, it also includes a cluster of homely residential and business streets. Here, one feels, is where the normal life of the principality is carried on. This is where the real Monegasques live and work. Sadly its scenic charm has suffered considerably from the proliferation of high-rise blocks around it. The railway station is on its landward side and the main coastal road, here the Boulevard Albert, passes through it.

Monte Carlo

In many ways the most enjoyable part of the principality is still Monte Carlo town with its pleasant streets, elegant shops, superb pastrycooks and, of course, exclusive hotels.

Monte Carlo is built on the Plâteau des Spélugues, the hill on the other side of the waterfront from Monaco. It acquired its name as recently as 1866, when Prince Charles III decided to call it 'Mount Charles' in Italian. The Plateau itself derives its name from the caves (Latin *spelunca*) at the foot of the rock and was at one time the property of an hotelier in Monaco. The purchase of the site was immediately followed by the creation of one of Europe's most confusingly named companies: the Société des Bains de Mers et du Cercle des Etrangers de Monaco (now known universally as the SBM). Anyone unfamiliar with Monaco might be forgiven for not knowing that the principal business of this 'Sea Bathing Company' is running the world-famous casinos. Its Foreigners Club angle is less stressed: it is hardly necessary with Monaco attracting a million visitors annually. The SBM has been controlled by the State of Monaco since l966, which owns 70 percent of the shares and Prince Rainier is its reigning tycoon.

The Casinos
There are three casinos in Monte Carlo: the Grand Casino, the Casino of the Sporting Club and the Casino Loews. But the first is the legendary one, with which the Theatre and the equally famous Hôtel du Paris are associated.

The Grand Casino, with a terrace overlooking the Mediterranean, inspired the 1920s song 'The Man who Broke the Bank at Monte Carlo': an Englishman called Charles Deville Wells reputedly won 1,000,000F in 1891. The Casino has recently been refurbished so that its elaborately stuccoed wedding-cake architecture conceals late 20th-century comforts. The splendid Salle Garnier was designed by Charles Garnier, architect of the Paris Opera. True, one-arm bandits and 'craps' have intruded on the classic gambling at roulette and chemin de fer, but otherwise it remains uniquely elegant. In the l960s the Greek shipowner Aristotle Onassis was a major shareholder in the SBM and once remarked to a guest, 'Can you imagine it? The Monegasques are people who run a casino at a loss.' Not any longer. Onassis himself is long gone, other merchant princes' yachts dominate the harbour, and under Prince Rainier's ultimate direction the Casino is booming. To get in you must be respectably dressed, have your passport and, if you are wise, obtain your entry ticket in the morning.

The Theatre
Adjacent to the Grand Casino on the main square, the Theatre was also partly designed by Garnier. Its most famous era was when the great director and impresario Diaghilev launched his Russian Ballet on its stage in the l920s. The Ballets Russes de Monte Carlo did much to create an audience for ballet in London.

The Principality of Monaco

Accommodation and Shopping
The Hôtel de Paris, the third of the *fin-de-siècle* triumvirate of buildings, along with the Casino and the Theatre, is the most famous and marginally the most expensive in Monte Carlo. Its Louis XV restaurant rates two Michelin stars. Rivalling it are the posh seafront Hôtel Loews and the Hermitage, but there are plenty of other establishments, though few cheap ones. A list can be had from the Tourist Office. One among many good restaurants is Chez Gianni, near the Hôtel de Paris. Naturally the town has branches of the most elegant Parisian shops and jewellers. It also hosts regular Sotheby's auctions of fine art since French auctioneering restrictions do not apply here.

Sports and Recreation
The most famous of local sporting events are the Monte Carlo Rally and the Monaco Grand Prix, which brings motor-racing enthusiasts from all over the world. The Grand Prix utilizes the winding streets of Monte Carlo as a circuit. This hair-raising event takes place in May.

The Monte Carlo Golf Club is 11 km (7 miles) along the main Nice road in France. Also 'abroad' is the beach, still largely the preserve of the wealthy, located 2½ km (1½ miles) east along the Corniche Inférieure towards Rocquebrune.

Beausoleil

If you feel that you cannot afford Monte Carlo prices, Beausoleil would make a good base for seeing the principality. As a resort it is well placed immediately behind and above Monte Carlo, and not too large with a 12,000 population. It was created in l903 out of part of La Turbie and is effectively an extension of upper Monte Carlo, from which it is separated by a symbolic frontier since it is in the French Alpes-Maritimes Department. There are spectacular views from the Mont des Mules above the town, reached by a short walk from the D53 which links the Moyenne Corniche with the higher Grande Corniche. It also has a number of good small hotels, notably the 2-star Olympia on the Bvd Général Leclerc. The Syndicat d'Initiative is in the Mairie.

La Turbie

Although not specifically allied to Monaco, except geographically, the small town of La Turbie is an absolute must to visit on account of its Roman remains and breathtaking views along the coast – haze permitting. It is 8 km (5 miles) from Monte Carlo up the hairpin bends of the D53. There is also a fine panorama from the Vistaero restaurant, further east along the Grande Corniche and 300 m (984 ft) above the sea.

Hôtel d'Alfonce, Pézenas

Languedoc

Mende to Narbonne

West of the Rhône Valley, between the Auvergne and the Mediterranean, lies some of the most beautiful, varied and in places mysterious countryside in the whole of France. Here in the remote inland areas of the Lozère and Gard departments are the dramatic gorges of the River Tarn and the Cévennes, the strange and desolate boulder-strewn plateaux called the Causses and mirage villages which turn out to be rock formations.

Eventually this barren landscape descends through stretches of harsh but fragrant moorland, sun-baked and bleached in some places, green and luxuriant in others, and sweeps down through olive and mulberry groves to vast vineyards and, eventually, salt-marshes, lagoons and the coastal resorts near Montpellier.

To the west of the Cévennes you come to the small town and château of Rouergue, the Aveyron River and the magnificent old town of Albi, birthplace of the artist Count Henri de Toulouse-Lautrec. This is an area that, though in the Midi-Pyrénées not

Languedoc, is well worth a protracted excursion as well as being accessible if you are coming to the Mediterranean through Toulouse by autoroute or train.

But first we shall take a look at the part most often visited: the landscapes of the Causses, the Gorges du Tarn, the National Park of the Cévennes and the country between them and the Rhône. A good detailed map is a necessity for exploring this area. One starting point could be Mende, situated just north of the Gorges du Tarn in the Lozère Department.

Mende

Apart from being a good place to base oneself, Mende is an agreeable small town, well situated in the upper valley of the River Lot. Its main sights are the cathedral, restored in the 17th century; the ancient bridge, the Pont Notre-Dame; and the museum of archaeology and folklore. There are magnificent views from the belvedere of nearby Mont Mimat.

The town has a population of 12,000, with appropriate shops and facilities and a variety of hotels, none of them expensive, the best being the Lion d'Or on the Bvd Britext (tel 66 49 16 46).

The Syndicat d'Initiative is at 16 Bvd du Soubeyran (tel 66 65 02 69) and can give useful advice on the best routes to the Cévennes and the Gorges du Tarn.

Florac and Routes to the Cévennes

From Mende take the N88 turning on to the N106 after 7½ km (4½ miles) to Florac, a distance of 39 km (24 miles), passing the panoramic views from the Col de Montmirat on the way to the plateau of the Causses. After the Col the road descends to the River Tarn and you can either go west to the Gorges du Tarn or continue to Florac itself and the magnificent Corniche du Cévennes.

Florac is a pleasant small town, at the foot of dolomite cliffs, with a few hotels and some furnished apartments available to rent. Its Tourist Office is on the Ave J.Monestier (tel 66 45 01 14).

Alternatively for the Gorges du Tarn you could go direct from Mende across the hills on the D986 to Ste Enimie and then along the Gorges to Le Rozier. But beware: any routes here will tempt you to stay on, because there is so much of beauty and interest to see.

The Causses

The product of something like 500 million years of strains and stresses in the earth, the Causses now present an extraordinary landscape of dry rocky plateaux through which the rivers Tarn, Jonte and Dourbie flow at the bottom of deep canyons and which are interspersed with fantastic grottoes and caves. The Causses' other startling characteristic is their extraordinary rock formations, which from a distance look so much like ancient villages that they have been given such names as Montpellier-le-Vieux and Nîmes-le-Vieux.

Location and Climate of the Causses

Geographically the Causses, which extend to the National Park of the Cévennes, lie between the towns of Mende to the north, Millau to the west and the Hérault Department to the south. The climate on the plateaux, which average about 1000 m (3280 ft) above sea-level, is hot and dry in summer and contrastingly harsh with a long snow season and strong winds in winter: nor is there much to temper the force of the wind. However, there have always been small villages and settlements in sheltered places, while sheep make the most of the sparse vegetation, providing wool for the textile industry of the towns and milk for the world-famous Roquefort cheese.

The Gorges of the Tarn

The canyons through which the main rivers flow offer some of the most awe-inspiring and dramatic landscapes in Europe and draw visitors from all over the world. But that should not put one off seeing the wonderful white limestone formations chiselled into fantastic shapes, a sort of mini Grand Canyon, where over millions of years the Tarn has carved its way down through the plateau.

Viewing Points

The most spectacular part of the Tarn gorges stretches some 35 km (22 miles) between the villages of Ste Enimie upstream and Le Rozier, with a minor road along the northern or right bank. Some of the best viewing points from which to look down into the gorges are the Cirque de St Chély and the Roc des Hourtous, both on the south bank near Ste Enimie, while the most famous is Point Sublime on the north bank, above the Cirque des Baumes (*cirque*, by the way, means a natural amphitheatre). To reach the latter from the south side, cross the river at Les Vignes and climb up the steep local road. You can also take boat trips on the river from La Malène, which lies between Ste Enimie and the Cirque des Baumes.

Tarn Region Villages
Ste Enimie is a typical old riverside village of the Lozère – the department through which the Tarn runs at this point – though with no hotels of note.

A little further downstream at St Chély-du-Tarn, a beautiful village in which motor traffic is prohibited, is the Auberge de la Cascade (tel 66 48 52 82). An old stone house, completely renovated, the Auberge has very reasonable prices and is open from 20 March to 30 September. Riding, swimming and canoeing on the Tarn are possible.

Then at La Malène, a tiny village, are two fine establishments, the Manoir de Montesquiou (tel 66 48 51 12) and the more expensive Château de la Caze (tel 66 48 51 01), the latter located 5 km (3 miles) back along the road to Ste Enimie.

At Le Rozier there are several hotels, notably the Grand Hôtel Muse et Rozier (tel 65 62 60 01), though the smaller Voyageurs (tel 65 62 60 09) is much cheaper.

Finally, downstream of the gorges is Millau, at the junction of the Tarn and the Dourbie rivers, with quite a number of hotels, including the pleasant Château de Creissels (tel 65 60 16 59) standing in its own park 2 km (1 mile) out on the Ste Affrique road.

Meyrueis

There is a lot to be said for basing yourself not actually on the Tarn, but at Meyrueis, on the uplands of the Causse Méjean between the Tarn and the Jonte rivers, and with easy access to all the area's sights including the gorges of both rivers and the greatest of the underground grottoes, the Aven Armand.

Meyrueis is a small town of only 1000 or so inhabitants, but with a number of hotels. The best, 1½ km (1 mile) outside it, is the Château d'Ayres (tel 66 45 60 10). This 18th-century château is very well placed in its own park up a small valley. It is furnished with antiques, offers an excellent restaurant and is by no means over-expensive. The Grand Hôtel Europe and its associated Mont Aigoual are cheaper, sharing gardens and a swimming-pool: a desirable feature in the heat of summer here. There is a Tourist Office in the old clock tower (tel 66 45 60 33).

The Causse Méjean

This highland area has two of the most spectacular of all the region's famous grottoes, Aven Armand and the Grotte de Dargilan. Over thousands of years, water finding its way down through the limestone of the Causses to an impermeable layer of rock has formed a whole underground network of caves, pools and streams, which emerge eventually as springs and waterfalls.

Aven Armand and other Grottoes

One of the greatest caves is Aven Armand, which is floodlit for visitors. It is also called the Forêt Vierge – petrified forest – because of its multitudinous and exotic 30 m (98 ft)-high stalagmites, columns built by limestone-saturated water dripping through the cavern's roof. The Grotte de Dargilan is a similar, though less large cave on the southern side of the River Jonte, entered through a rock-face above the river. Other well known ones are the Grotte des Demoiselles, a 50 m (164 ft)-high cavern near Ganges with a natural scuplture known as the Virgin and Child; the Abîme de Bramabiau near the River Trévézel, which includes caves and a subterranean river; and the Grotte de Clamouse near St Guilhem-le-Désert.

Hyelgas Rural Museum

Some 6 km (4 miles) from Meyruis is a small rural-life museum in an old farmhouse. With its old photographs, farm carts and mementoes of a past life this gives a very good sense of the bleak and desolate existence involved with farming these uplands in the early 20th century.

Gorges de la Dourbie

South of the Tarn, which the River Dourbie joins at Millau, are the Gorges de la Dourbie, comparable in splendour to those of the Tarn, if less celebrated. Not far from the rivers' confluence is one of the most famous of those hilltop rock formations that look like villages, namely Montpellier-le-Vieux.

The 'Chaos' of Montpellier-le-Vieux

The full name of this rock formation gives a good idea of the appearance of its spectacular 'natural ruins'. They are said to have been brought about by the association, in the same rock masses, of both soluble calcium carbonate and insoluble magnesium carbonate. Water finding its way through the soluble parts has eroded those, but not the hard rock, thus carving out extraordinary 'ruined' towers, arcades, bluffs and alleyways. At the same time the clay residue from the soluble material has given a foothold to vegetation, which adds charm and verisimilitude to the 'ruined village'. Montpellier-le-Vieux stands 18 km (11 miles) north-east of Millau and can only be visited from the Maubert café-restaurant, which is off the D111 road from Millau. There you must buy an entry ticket, which allows you to drive about a mile along a private road to a vast parking lot, from where you can explore the site on foot.

Other 'Natural Villages'
Other well known examples of this geological phenomenon in the region are at Nîmes-le-Vieux, Arcs-de-St-Pierre, Ruquesaltes and Rajol; while much further south at the Cirque de Moureze, 8 km (5 miles) west of Clermont l'Herault, the ancient village of Moureze actually stands among the enormous dolomite rocks of a 'natural village'.

Cévennes National Park

East of the Gorges de la Dourbie is the Cévennes National Park, into which the River Trévézel flows and which is bounded on the north-east by the celebrated Corniche des Cévennes. The park is noted for its flora and fauna. Since the end of the 19th century systematic reforestation has largely compensated for the earlier destruction of the woodlands both by charcoal burners, who caused havoc among the beech trees, and by the great flocks of sheep which cropped the young leaves and shoots in their seasonal migrations from the lower Languedoc to the Cévennes. Today the area has recovered and its little-used roads offer plenty to explore among its small mountains and high prairies, with lots of flowers including lovely purple orchids.

If you are interested in the character of the Cévennes you could do much worse than prepare yourself by reading Robert Louis Stevenson's classic, *Travels with a Donkey*. Neither tourism nor modern roads have yet altered the countryside sufficiently to make his observations invalid, even if the once legendary 'Beast of Gevaudon' no longer roams the hills and forests.

Mountains and the Corniche
The highest peak in the park is Mont Aigoual (1567 m/5140 ft),

Languedoc

offering panoramic views from its observatory when the weather is right (its height is matched by its rainfall). Mont Lozère, not in the park but to the north beyond the Corniche, is higher at 1702 m (5582 ft) and also has notable views. The Corniche itself runs from Florac, on the Gorges du Tarn, a distance of 53 km (33 miles) through spectacular scenery down to St Jean du Gard.

Le Mas de Sobeyran
Near St Jean du Gard is Le Mas de Soubeyran, a museum dedicated to the rebellion of the Camisards of the Cévennes during the early days of Protestantism in France.

Routes South from the Cévennes
From St Jean du Gard you leave the Cévennes and can either continue east to the famous Pont du Gard, the captivating town of Uzès and Nîmes; or continue south towards Montpellier and the Mediterranean. This latter route from St Jean du Gard goes over the Col de l'Asclier, with superb views but hair-raising bends, to the valley of the River Herault, passing near the Grotte des Demoiselles, St Guilhelm-le-Désert and the Grotte de Clamouse.

South of the Cévennes the country changes rapidly. You do not have to travel far from the high plateaux to reach an agreeable countryside of oaks, heather, chestnut forests and small villages, after which the lower valleys lead to the vineyards and olive groves, the lavender and wild herbs of the Mediterranean.

St Guilhem-le-Désert

The tiny village of St Guilhem-le-Désert lies just over 32 km (20 miles) from Montpellier in the Hérault Department. With its abbey-church dating from the 11th century, square tower, Roman houses and the remains of its surrounding ramparts, it is one of the jewels of southern France. At the confluence of the Verdus and the Hérault rivers, it is in a region of splendid gorges and has a backcloth of scarps dominated by the Château de Don Juan (or Château du Géant, as it is sometimes called).

The Abbey
The abbey, round which the village is clustered, was founded in 804 by Guilhem, Duke of Acquitaine – the Guilhem d'Orange of the *Chansons de Geste* – but all that remains is the church, which was consecrated in 1076. Its splendid doorway, which faces a square shaded by a massive 100-year-old plane tree, is crowned by a 15th-century bell-tower. The great apse, with its lovely colonnade under the tiled roof and its elegant supporting apses

on either side, is a blend of strength and elegance, and both the abbey-church and the surrounding houses are warm and radiant in gold-coloured stone with red and ochre roofs.

La Grotte de Clamouse
For the grotto-seeker, Clamouse is 3 km (2 miles) away to the south of St Guilhem along the D4. It is noted for its weirdly formed and strangely coloured stalactites. The grottoes of the Sergeant and Beaume Celliler are just over 3 km (2 miles) away – *plus* a total of about six hours' walking (there and back) when you leave the D4. The path is on the left just over a mile after leaving St Guilhem in the direction of Ganges and Montpellier.

Cirque de Navacelles and Cirque de Moureze
The Cirque des Navacelles, north of St Guilhem and the Cirque de Moureze south of the village, are natural amphitheatres. The former is far above the bends of a river below; the latter, as already mentioned, forms a 'chaos' of house-like rocks around the real village of Moureze.

Accommodation
Accommodation is fairly sparse around here. St Guilhem has one small hotel, La Taverne de l'Escuelle (67 52 72 05) which would make an excellent base for exploring the area, but you are not likely to find a room vacant if you arrive without warning between May and September. Distinctly more grand, and a considerable distance away on the D25 between Ganges and the Cirque de Navacelles, is the 16th-century Château de Madières (tel 67 73 84 03). Set in its own park, the château has been sensitively converted into a hotel and is not expensive for what it offers.

From this area you can either take the road to the small town of Clermont L'Hérault, *en route* to Pézenas and Beziers or swing east again to Montpellier, Nîmes and the Languedoc coast adjacent to the Camargue. We deal with Pézenas and Beziers last.

Montpellier

Montpellier, in some ways one of the most pleasing cities of the South, is also one of the most interesting in its combination of historic interest and contemporary dynamism. The medieval heart of the old city, deeply scarred by the French Wars of Religion, became the administrative capital of Languedoc under Louis XIV and was enriched with some of the most elegant town houses – or *hôtels particuliers* – in France in a veritable sunburst of contained urban development. In our own time, while the old

Languedoc

city has been preserved for both day-to-day use and aesthetic enjoyment, the commercial, industrial, residential and educational sectors have been developed to meet a population growth of over 36 percent in the past decade.

What this means to the quality of the city as a place to visit includes the sense of youth and vitality given by not only one great university (with memories of Rabelais), but three, attended by something like 45,000 students. There is also a new administrative centre only a few hundred yards from the old city in which the elegance of the new Mairie makes it a classic of modern architecture. A series of residential and research centres encircle the old town, each of which contributes its own sense of architectural and social stimulus, particularly Ricardo Boffi's Antigone, the neo-classical residential centre whose central square is often alive with the sounds of artisans' stalls and jazz. The very efficient SI is situated near the Place de la Comédie (tel 67 58 26 04).

The Peyrou and Aqueduct
For holidays and leisure travel generally, Montpellier has much to offer – not least an average of 300 sunny days a year and a mild winter. It is essentially a southern town with all the facilities for spending much of one's life in the open air that that description implies. From the huge main square, the Place de la Comédie – the largest pedestrian square in Europe – a maze of busy narrow old streets concealing many fine old *hôtels particuliers* climb to the highest point of the city, which is crowned by an elegant, rectangular tree-lined terrace: the Peyrou. There is a local legend that the name comes from the old word for a heap of stones, and was first used to describe the site by the townspeople while the monumental terrace was being cleared and built during the 18th century. At the eastern end of the terrace is a magnificent triumphal arch in honour of Louis XIV, in the middle an equestrian statue of the same monarch, and at the western end an impressive 18th-century water-tower, or *château d'eau*. This water-tower marks the Montpellier end of a remarkable aqueduct, 880 metres (over half a mile) long and 22 metres (over 70 ft) high, which strides over the western outskirts of the city to bring water from a source at St Clement and elsewhere. Built in the 18th century in two superimposed arcades, and inspired by the Pont du Gard, it is a dramatic sight to come across, whether first seen from the Peyrou or from the streets below.

The best time to climb the hill to the Peyrou (with its east-west axis) and to stroll along its walks – sometimes to the accompaniment of music from concealed sources in the gardens – is the evening. For at this time the triumphal arch, which marks the highest point of the old city, is ablaze with the sunset. Alternatively, visit it after dark when the arch and *château d'eau* are floodlit. Near the Peyrou is the Jardin des Plantes – France's first botanical garden, designed in 1593.

The Musée Fabre
The Fabre museum has an impressive collection of 19th- and early 20th-century French paintings. Frédéric Bazille, the French Impressionist painter who at one time looked after the young, impoverished Renoir, and whose tall figure is seen among the painters in *The Studio at the Batignolles* painted by Fantin-Latour in 1870 and now in the Louvre, is well represented in the museum. But check first whether his canvases are there or on loan to some other gallery in France. Even if they are missing, there is a marvellous cool Matisse, and some fine Corots and Courbets to console you.

Festivals
The principal festivals are the dance festival in June/July followed by the international jazz festival. These are held respectively in the Theatre Municipal, Place de la Comédie, and the Château d'O, about 4 km (3 miles) north-west of the city centre.

Accommodation and Restaurants
Montpellier's foremost hotel is the 4-star Métropole (tel 67 58 11 22) in Rue Clos René closely followed by a number of 3-star establishments such as the Hôtel de Noailles (tel 67 60 49 80) and Sofitel (tel 67 58 45 45), all of which are fairly central, the Noailles being in the quiet of the Rue Ecoles-Centrales. The Métropole offers both swimming and tennis. For those on a tighter budget there is no shortage of 2-, 1- or no-star places which generally have rooms free even during the festivals, though it is advisable to book early in the day. Of these try the 2-star Les Myrtes (tel 67 42 60 11) or, by the Jardin des Plantes, the Hôtel Les Fauvettes (tel 67 63 17 60). There is also the youth hostel (tel 67 79 61 66) and, in a converted mansion in the old town, a place called the Foyer des Jeunes Travailleuses (tel 67 52 83 11) run along similar lines.

The best of Montpellier's restaurants is the Chandelier (tel 67 92 61 62) in Rue Leenhardt. The cafés of the Place de la Comédie make a pleasant place to relax accompanied by the playing of the square's fountains.

Two points to watch in Montpellier. Be wary of the one-way traffic system in the outer boulevards, which, if you are not on the alert,

Languedoc

may have you circling the centre of the town many times before
you spot your turn into the old city. Also, do not be misled by the
brave blue appearance on maps of the River Verdanson, a
tributary of the Lez near the northern boundary of the old city: it is
an empty, high-walled river-bed – empty, that is, except for the
rubbish dumped in it.

Nîmes

If you drive to Nîmes from Montpellier by the N113 (52 km/32½
miles) through Verdargues, Lunel and Milhaud there is nothing,
particularly in the last few miles, to prepare you for the magnificence that is Nîmes itself. True, you drive through apparently
endless vineyards (competing with each other in their invitations
to stop and taste the local product), but the last stretch is a
gauntlet of road signs, massive billboards, petrol stations,
garages, industrial sites and shacks, culminating in a residential
industrial belt of total anonymity but unmistakably recent date.

Moreover, if you arrive in the Montpellier bus, except for an
impressive glimpse of the Avenue Feuchères there is not a great
deal, up to the moment you step off the bus, to indicate that you
are only an easy stroll from some of the most exciting vistas in
Europe. The SI is at 6 Rue Auguste (tel 66 67 29 11).

The Arènes
A few minutes' walk past the Esplanade and the Palais de Justice
brings you to the Arènes – the best preserved of all the 70 Roman
amphitheatres still to be found in the world.

The first glimpse of the great amphitheatre makes a curious
impression. For one thing, there is enough open space around for
one to be able to see it in something like perspective, and further,
the sandy waste immediately close to it seems both ancient and
homely for the marshalling of vast numbers of spectators who
gather for the *corridas* that are held throughout the summer. All
this, together with posters announcing forthcoming *ferias* which
include both bullfights and *courses à la cocarde* (competitions to
seize a rosette from the bull's horns and get away with it safely),
creates an intimate, lived-in atmosphere round this incredible
monument which seems to conjure up the approaches of a
football stadium rather than the relics of a centre of ancient
blood-sports. Indeed, for those who would like to see it put to a
better human use than bull-baiting, it is ironical to recall that at
one period in its long history the amphitheatre was seized by
poor squatters, who borrowed materials from the great mass of

Roman masonry to build themselves homes and a chapel. The village in the arena at one time had 2000 inhabitants, and it was not until the 19th century that the debris of this occupation was finally cleared away.

The Arènes is also the venue for the town's jazz festival that takes place during the second week of July, preceded by an opera production and a rock concert. The SI can provide a listing for all events occuring during this frenetic period.

The Maison Carrée
The Maison Carrée, a pleasantly domesticated mini-Parthenon, now crowded-in a little by some of the city's most charming streets, has an appeal that owes less to Roman pomp, efficiency and brutality than to Greek inspiration softened and humanized in the sun of southern France. There is a small but admirable selection of items inside the building, which provide a foretaste, or an extension, of the excellent Archaeological Museum in a former Jesuit college off the Bvd Admiral-Courbet.

Other Attractions
Nîmes, which gave its name to the fabric denim (de Nîmes), is a city in and around which one could easily spend a whole summer. The Fountain Gardens, created on the slopes of Mont Cavalier in the 18th century and crowned by La Tour Magne, probably France's most ancient monument, are cool and beautifully designed. The streets are magnificent and tree-lined, or intimate and charming, like those near the Maison Carrêe. In the same area you may, if you are fortunate, stumble on a pastrycook's shop selling croquants de Villaret (dry almond cookies). Other local delicacies are pickled olives and caladons (almond cakes).

Nîmes is also within easy reach of the Pont du Gard, that most majestic Roman aqueduct and there is an 18-hole golf course, plus stables, roughly 11 km (7 miles) south of the city at Camp-agne just off the D42. (18 km (11 miles) south-west of Nîmes is the Perrier Source Minerale – an underground lake from which over 700 million bottles per year are filled.)

Accommodation
Nîmes is a particularly good base for touring the countryside because of the number and variety of the hotels, ranging from the 4-star L'Imperator (tel 66 21 90 30), which boasts a fine garden and superb restaurant, and the excellent Hôtel du Cheval Blanc (tel 66 67 20 03) opposite the Arène, through a good selection of medium-priced hotels to many other modest but comfortable

establishments. The 2-star Hôtel de la Maison Carrée (tel 66 67 32 89) is delightfully situated if you like to stay in the very heart of a city you are visiting for the first time. The Nouvel Hôtel (tel 66 67 62 48) and Hôtel de France (tel 66 67 23 05) both offer value-for-money accommodation. There is also a good youth hostel (tel 66 23 25 04) north-west of the city centre that allows some camping.

Uzès

Uzès is a charming and relaxed town now largely restored to the medieval splendour it enjoyed when the royal family of the Crussol d'Uzès ruled from the ducal palace – the Duché d'Uzès. The local SI can be found in the Place de la Libération (tel 66 22 68 88).

The Fenestrelle Tower
Centred around the Place aux Herbes – the site of a lively Saturday market – the old quarter can be identified from a series of towers the most remarkable of which, and unique to France, is the six-storey fenestrated bell-tower of the Cathedral. This, the Fenestrelle Tower, is all that remains of the 12th-century Romanesque cathedral razed in the course of the Wars of Religion. Its replacement, the Cathedrale St Theodorit, has little of note beyond its organ, which retains its painted shutters and dates from the 17th century. Unfortunately the bell-tower is not open to the public.

The Duché
The Duché can be visited for a small charge. A mishmash of styles with a superimposed but well proportioned Renaissance front façade, the Duché has an interesting Gothic chapel. Inside are paintings, tapestries and much of the original period furniture. The Tour Bermonde gives a commanding view of the Garrigues.

Uzès also lends itself to idle walks through the old streets, the detailed architecture of the frontages and the narrow, winding passages giving a greater sense of oneness with the ancient sites. From the remains of the town walls are splendid views up to the Garrigues or down to the river. Further afield there are the Ardèche and the Pont du Gard to explore.

Festivals
Early August sees the celebration of the town's patron saint's day, with bulls running in the streets and free-flowing *pastis* in the bars. A more sober event is the annual music festival – the Nuits Musicales d'Uzès – held in late July. Information on all festivals

and excursions into the surrounding countryside can be obtained
from the Syndicat d'Initiative.

Accommodation
Far and away the best hotel in the area is the Hôtel Marie d'Agoult
in the Château d'Arpaillargues (tel 66 22 14 48) situated 4½ km (3
miles) west of Uzès (D982). It has a tennis court, a swimming-
pool, a lovely garden and a very good restaurant. For places in
Uzes itself, it is probably best to check with the SI who will
provide a list, particularly for those looking for a campsite or
cheaper accommodation. The town's 3-star hotel is the Entrai-
gues (tel 66 22 32 68). The Auberge de St Maximine provides a
pleasant atmosphere and you can eat out in the courtyard.

The Garrigues

The Garrigues form an arid, herb- and scrub-covered expanse of
exposed limestone and picturesque gorges, most notably the
Gorges du Gardon. To see the best of the gorge, leave Nîmes for
Uzès by the D979 that runs roughly due north between the two
towns over a distance of 25 km (16 miles). Scenic for most of its
length, the views surpass themselves as the road winds down
through a series of hairpin bends to the Pont St Nicholas over the
River Gardon (or Gard). The bridge, a 13th-century, seven-arched
construction, also affords fine views.

The Pont du Gard

The Pont du Gard is easily reached from Uzès by the D981 – a
distance of roughly 15 km (9 miles). Alternatively it is 25 km (15½
miles) by the N100 then D981 from Avignon, or 23 km (14 miles)
by the N86 and D981 after Remoulins from Nîmes.

Once part of a 48 km (30 mile) aqueduct built by Agrippa in 19BC
to supply Nîmes with water, the Pont du Gard now stands in
splendid isolation. Rising 40 m (130 ft) above the River Gardon,
its perfection belies its 2000 years – albeit with a little help from
Napoleon III's restoration in the 19th century. Built in three tiers of
stone blocks weighing up to 6 tons each, only the top tier carried
any water. You can now walk down the covered canal where once
up to 44 million gallons of water coursed each day. But before
climbing up the path to gain access to the top tier it is well worth
walking a further 100 yards or so upstream towards the Château
St Privat for a superb view of the aqueduct from the banks of the
river.

The Languedoc Coast

From La Grande Motte, on the edge of the Camargue, down to Port Leucate and indeed beyond, the sandy beaches of Languedoc witnessed a surge of development during the l970s and 1980s as a result of a French Government development plan initiated in l963. Most of the resultant resorts are far from rivalling the Côte d'Azur in sophistication. But they serve families well because they are not as expensive as the Riviera, have less pollution and excellent facilities for watersports, as well as summer nightlife. However, you only reach a coastline of individual character right down near the Spanish frontier on Roussillon's celebrated Côte Vermeille. This is described in the next chapter. Here we deal with the Languedoc resorts most easily reached via Montpellier Airport or, if you are travelling by train, via the ancient and interesting towns of Pézenas, Beziers and Narbonne.

La Grande Motte

One of the first of the purpose-built resorts on this coast, the pyramidal blocks of holiday apartments known as La Grande Motte were designed by the architect Jean Balladur to resemble temples of the sun, which would also screen the beaches from the prevailing wind. On a recent visit, however, some of these monstrous edifices had begun to deteriorate. None the less the beaches remain excellent as does the golf course. There are also berths for over 1000 yachts in the three basins of the port and some first-class hotels, notably the small and expensive Grand M'Hotel (tel 67 29 13 13) and the much larger Altea (tel 67 56 90 81). Various cheaper hotels without restaurants include the Golf (tel 67 29 72 00). They all close in January and some through from November to Easter. The Alexandre restaurant (tel 67 56 63 63) has been recommended though it was closed during our visit. Parallel developments near La Grande Motte are Port Camargue to the east and Carnon to the west.

Continuing down the coast past the huge lagoons is impossible beyond the old fishing port of Palavas, except by boat. You have to drive inland towards Montpellier, pick up the autoroute briefly and then branch off on the N112 for the pleasant old town and port of Sète.

Sète

In many ways Sète is a reminder of the kind of family holiday places many of us knew when we were very young – a fishing port, set below an old town on a hill. Technically an island, it is joined up to the beaches on both sides by bridges and was first thought of as a port by King Henri IV, though construction did not start until I666. Ever since then it has had a working harbour though the heavy ship traffic goes to the new commercial port nearby. The Office de Tourisme is at 60 Grand Rue Mario-Roustan (tel 67 74 71 71) in the heart of the old town.

The Old Town
Sète was the birthplace of the writer Paul Valéry and a museum commemorates him and contains exhibits on the history of Sète. There are plenty of shops, hotels and restaurants, especially along the canal running into the old port. A good place to observe the hustle and bustle of the waterfront is from the pleasant Hôtel de l'Orque Bleu on the Quai de l'Aspirant Herber.

The Battle of the Barges
As well as the old port being busy with a wide variety of vessels, from trawlers to pleasure craft, it is also the scene of an annual spectacle called *les joutes* in which two gaily decorated barges fight a battle for each crew of oarsmen to board the others boat.

Mont St Clair
The hill that makes such an appealing backdrop to the town, Mont St Clair, reaches a height of 175 m (570 ft) and is accessible by a variety of paths. There is also an excursion route of some 8 km (5 miles) around the hill.

Accommodation
There are numerous small hotels in the town. The Orque Bleu (tel 67 74 72 13), already mentioned, is a reasonably priced good hotel, though without a restaurant. Out on the Corniche along the N112 there are also a number of beach hotels, none of them large. The excellent beaches continue the whole 20 km (12 miles) to Cap d'Agde, part of a narrow strip of land between the sea and the lagoon called the Bassin de Thau.

Cap d'Agde

One of the seven modern resorts created along this coast as a result of the 1963 development plan, Cap d'Agde is considerably more appealing than La Grande Motte, and also incorporates an old port. In fact it has three parts: Old Agde, Le Grau d'Agde and Cap d'Agde. Old Agde, with its cathedral made of volcanic rock, is fascinating. Situated slightly inland, the River Hérault flows past it to debouch at Le Grau d'Agde, the old harbour that still has all the paraphernalia of a fishing village. Cap d'Agde, the modern resort, is on the promontory where a port was first conceived on the orders of the Duc de Richelieu. It has been designed like a typical Mediterranean fishing village and the colours and shapes on the waterfront, although the buildings are concrete, are charming and relaxed. The SI is on the Rue L-Bages (tel 67 94 29 68).

Further down the coast, past Valras Plage and Narbonne Plage, is Gruissan, on the border of ancient Roussillon.

Gruissan

Gruissan is another modern development attractively designed to exploit the beaches around an old fishing port. Lying between two lagoons on what is almost an island site, and linked with the sea by a canal, the old red-roofed village clusters around the slopes of a rock on which stand the remains of Barbarossa's Tower. The village, with its own port and boatyard, and a small military museum, has several pleasant restaurants. The SI is on Les Hublots du Port (tel 68 49 03 25) in the village. Five minutes' walk away is the beach resort, with its apartment blocks, yacht harbour and the excellent 2-star Hôtel Corail (tel 68 49 04 43).

To drive further south along the coast you must go inland to Narbonne, skirting the huge lagoon of Bages and Sigean.

Port Leucate

A whole stretch of the Roussillon coast north of Perpignan, from La Franqui to Port Barcarès, is effectively one tourist develop-ment, with Port Leucate at its centre. As a holiday-resort complex it is one of the most ambitious in France, with quays, yacht berths, canals, apartment clusters, small houses, hotels and shopping centres on what was once a mosquito-plagued no man's land between the Leucate lagoon and the sea. With the mosquitoes eliminated, these vast sandy beaches have come into their own. There is hot sun with some wind to temper it, a magnificent fusion of land and water and easy access to the Corbières with that region's vineyards, hills and ancient castles.

Architecturally there is a confusion of styles. But for family holidays these apartment 'villages' offer considerable comfort and convenience, while the landscape gardening of Port Leucate is as imaginative as the design of the port and yacht basin. There is every kind of sport available, excellent shops and other acco-modation from 2-star hotels to campsites. The principal SI is at the Centre Polyvalent, Port Leucate (tel 68 40 91 31).

Pézenas

Among the inland diversions on the way south from Montpellier is the small town of Pézenas, attractively set among vineyards only 25 km (16 miles) from Cap d'Agde. A fortified town under the Romans, it later became an important wool-trading centre, with three annual fairs. After 1456 it was the seat of the Governors of Languedoc, the Montmorencys and the Contis. More directly interesting is the town's association with the playwright Molière, whose *Le Médecin Volant* was first performed here before the Prince de Conti and his court in 1650. Indeed he was given the title and privileges of 'Actor to the Prince de Conti'.

The SI is imaginatively installed in what was once the barber Gély's shop in the old Marche au Bled, where Molière – according to tradition – spent many hours in the wig-maker's comfortable chairs, taking part in the customers' conversations.

The superb 17th-century houses and courtyards of the old town are clearly but unobtrusively signposted, so that a tour is simple and agreeable. One of the most notable buildings is the Hôtel d'Alfonce, where Molière's plays are reputed to have been performed in the loggia. Others are the Renaissance Hôtel de Lacoste and the Hôtel de Wicque. Markets are held in the Cours Jean-Jaurès, where there are various cafés. Every summer the 'Mirondela des Arts' is held in the shops, galleries, workrooms and streets of the town, with exhibitions, music, craft demonstrations and general celebrations.

Béziers

A town with 85,000 inhabitants, ten times the size of Pézenas, Béziers is by origin pre-Roman. In 1209 its Catholic population resisted a religious crusade by the Albigeois – part of the complicated wars caused by the Cathar heresy in this region – and a horrific massacre ensued. Béziers was burnt to the ground, although parts of the ancient Cathedral of St Nazaire survived.

Today Bêziers' prosperity depends on wine. It has a large number of hotels and many restaurants. The Office du Tourisme is at 27 Rue Quatre-Septembre (tel 67 49 24 19). The airport has scheduled internal flights and the great Canal du Midi passes just south of the town on its way to the sea near Agde.

Canals
The low lying land between Béziers and Narbonne, and down to

the coast, is criss-crossed with an intricate system of waterways. The famous Canal du Midi goes alongside the River Aude to Carcassonne, eventually joining with the River Garonne and reaching Bordeaux. At this end it links with the Canal de la Robine, going down past Narbonne to Port Nouvelle on the Mediterranean. Canal boats and cabin-cruisers can be hired for expeditions as long – or as short – as you want to make them. Names of boat-hire companies specializing in this area are available from French National Tourist Offices, which publish 'Special Interest Holiday' brochures.

Narbonne

Waking up after an overnight train journey from Paris, Narbonne is one of those places where you are sure you are in the South. The red-tiled roofs, the scents, the sun: all proclaim it. For many motorists it is merely a stop *en route* to Spain. But this ancient city, founded by the Romans in AD 118 and later the seat of the Visigoth kings, is attractive in its own right. The Cathedral with its tapestries of the Creation, the Cour de la Madeleine in the Old Palace, the modest Archbishop's Palace, the Dungeon of Gilles Aycelin and the central Place de l'Hôtel de Ville are all well worth seeing. The SI is in the Place R. Salengro (tel 68 65 15 60), near the Maison Vigneronne – wine is as important to Narbonne as it is to Béziers. There are a number of comfortable hotels, while Le Réverbère restaurant has earned two stars from Michelin.

Narbonne Plage, 15 km (10 miles) from the town, is a modern resort with its own hotels.

Minerve and the Minervois

One of the largest wine-growing areas in the locality is up in the hills of the Minervois. It is also worth an expedition to see the ancient hill-town of Minerve itself. Built on a site fortified by nature on a dramatic rock promontory, Minerve was a centre of the Cathar heretics. It was bloodily besieged by Simon de Montfort in 12l0, after which 100 of the Cathar leaders were thrown from the cliff.

Sigean African Reserve

On the Bages and Sigean Lagoon there is an African Wildife Reserve, reached by the N9 road going south. Antelope, lion and white rhino are among the species kept here, and pink flamingos, pelicans and other waterbirds can be found on the lagoon. The Reserve is 17 km (11 miles) from Narbonne.

Monastery of St Martin-de-Canigou

Roussillon

Nestling in the foothills of the Pyrenees, with the Corbières hills jutting out from them to hem in the coastal plain around Perpignan, Roussillon has for countless centuries been a cultural and military crossroads. Near Perpignan stands the 15th-century fortress of Salses, guarding the all-important route down the coast to Catalonia. Further north, the legendary ramparts of Carcassonne survey the wide valley of the River Aude, which divides Roussillon from the Minervois mountains of lower Languedoc.

There is always a penalty for living astride a major strategic route. The inhabitants of Roussillon have been hearing the tramp of invading armies since long before the birth of Christ. In the 2nd Century BC the region belonged to the Roman province of the Narbonnaise – as is recounted in the history of Perpignan below – and Hannibal marched through in AD 214 on his way to campaign in Spain, following the Roman road past Salses. Six centuries later the Emperor Charlemagne was doing the same, as a result of Roussillon becoming a bone of contention between France and

Roussillon

Spain. It was ruled from Aragon and later by the Kings of Majorca, during the 12th to 14th centuries, when incessant pressures from the Counts of Toulouse were leading to sieges of Carcassonne. The incorporation of the province into the Kingdom of France was only finally achieved with the Treaty of the Pyrenees in 1659, following the last siege of Perpignan in 1742. It is thus entirely appropriate to start a visit to the region with Carcassonne.

Carcassonne

The first sight of Carcassonne is unforgettable. Whether approaching by train or road in the half-light of early morning, the outline of the old city in the distance is a remarkable spectacle. Even today neither crowds nor trinket shops can destroy the beauty and power of this unique survival.

For visitors old and new the Syndicat d'Initiative (tel 68 25 07 04) is in Boulevard Camille Pelletan, though there is a sub-office at the Porte Narbonnaise (tel 68 25 68 81) open in July and August only. The main office can also be used for information and booklets on the Aude Department.

La Cité
The Old Town, La Cité, stands on an escarpment on the right bank of the River Aude from where its fantastical, Disney-like outline dominates the approach to it over the two bridges, the Ponts Neuf and Vieux, from the lower town or Ville Basse. This structure is the most remarkable fortified enclosure in Europe. One of the world's greatest gifts to historians and archeologists, it ranges from huge Gallo-Roman stone blocks securely interlocked, and without mortar, to the Royal Walls of rectangular grey stones of the age of St Louis. Within this range there are the cubic stones of the Visigoths, alternating with brick courses, and, from ducal times, sandstone blocks assembled in roughly shaped masses. And if the centuries appear to have become mixed, much of this was due to the excavation, and removal to other parts, of the structure of lower depths of walling during the creation of the upper and lower tiltyards.

The site of the old city attracted the Romans from the 1st century BC because of its commanding position between the Mediterranean and Toulouse. The Visigoths seized it for the same reason in the 5th century AD and built a new defensive wall from which the line of towers seen today is derived. Three centuries later it was the turn of the Franks followed by the counts of Toulouse under whom Carcassonne enjoyed 400 years as a prosperous local capital. That lasted until the 13th century, when its peace was broken by the Crusade against the Albigensians, which brought so much devastation and bloodshed to Languedoc, where the religious reform movement was strongest.

200,000 Frenchmen from the north, under the command of Simon de Montfort, prepared to drive the 'heretics' from Languedoc, and after sacking Beziers, laid siege to Carcassonne in 1209. The defence of the city was organized by Count Raymond VI de Toulouse and his 24-year-old son Raymond-Roger. Raymond-Roger, lured from the fortress to negotiate with a false promise of safe conduct, was seized as soon as he reached De Montfort's camp, chained and thrown into prison. The defenders of Carcassonne, near to famine, lost heart and De Montfort seized the city, where Raymond-Roger died six months later, prisoner in a dungeon of his own city.

After a futile attempt in 1240 by Raymond-Roger's son to regain the city, Louis XI of France (St Louis) caused the houses which had been built at the foot of the ramparts to be razed to the ground and the rebellious inhabitants paid for their loyalty with seven years' expulsion to the other side of the river, where they built what is now the Ville Basse. From then on, directed by St Louis' son, the Old Town became an impregnable fortress self-sufficient in food and water – the Narbonne Tower holding a six-month supply. At this time the second wall, the St Nazaire cathedral and the open-air theatre were also added.

During the Hundred Years War the Black Prince had to give up any idea of taking the city and be content with setting fire to the Ville Basse. After 1659, with Roussillon annexed to France, not Carcassonne but Perpignan became the frontier defence against Spain, and the city might well have been allowed to decline, or even to be demolished. With the revival of interest in the Middle Ages during the 19th century, however, the French government entrusted the restoration of Carcassonne to Viollet-le-Duc, and the work continues today. Although much criticized for a few of his excesses – such as the addition of crenellations in a Visigoth style at odds with the rest of St Nazaire cathedral's architecture, and blue tiles for the inner towers – Viollet-le-Duc had an undeniable mastery of medieval construction techniques and should also be thanked for restoring the city's skyline to its former romantic jostle of towers and turrets.

La Cité can be entered by either the Porte d'Aude on the west side, leaving your car near the church of St Gimer, or on the east side through the Porte Narbonnaise where entry, again on foot from the large car parks nearby, is over a drawbridge. The upper and lower tiltyards can be visited without charge – a stroll there gives excellent views of the city. For the Château Comtal and the inner towers you have to take a guided tour.

The Ville Basse
The lower town, or Ville Basse, should not be ignored or altogether overshadowed by the older part, La Cité. There is a good collection of paintings from the 17th and 18th centuries (including some Chardin still-lifes) in the Musée des Beaux Arts, Rue de Verdun, which also has interesting material relating to André Chenier, the revolutionary poet whose childhood was spent in Carcassonne and who died on the scaffold in 1794. The lower town also incorporates the ancient commercial and bourgeois districts, with its main boulevards on the lines of the old ramparts.

Accommodation
Carcassonne itself has no 4-star hotel, though 2½ km (1½ miles) south-east by the D118 and D104 is the Domaine d'Auriac (tel 68 25 72 22), a charming 19th-century building set in gardens with tennis courts and a swimming-pool. Within the Cité are the 3-star Donjon (tel 68 71 08 80) and Hôtel des Remparts (tel 68 71 27 72), but generally for value for money it is better to stick to the Ville Basse. The exception is the youth hostel (tel 68 25 23 16) in Rue de Vicomte Trencavel. In the Ville Basse try the 3-star Terminus (tel 68 25 25 00) or, less expensive but tidy and with a good-value restaurant, the 1-star Hôtel Cathare (tel 68 25 65 92).

Restaurants
Restaurants in the Cité are not as expensive as one might imagine, but they may be shut out of season. Le Sénéchal, in Rue Viollet-le-Duc, allows you to eat in the romantic setting of its courtyard. In the Ville Basse, the restaurants along the Boulevard Omer Sarraut are a good place to start looking for a simple meal. More upmarket is the Languedoc in Allée d'Iena, and do try the local speciality of *cassoulet*, a stew of white beans, herbs and meat.

From Carcassone, Perpignan lies 118 km (74 miles) away by the D118 and N117 which will take you through the heart of the Corbières, past the perilously sited châteaux of Peyrepertuse and Quéribus. Alternatively the Corbières can be skirted by taking the N113 to Narbonne then the N9 down the coast to Perpignan, a quicker journey but one which can be extended to include the

Abbaye de Fontfroide and the Fort de Salses, both well worth the extra mileage and time. The autoroutes A61 and A9 mirror this latter route.

The Corbières

Through the Corbières is one of the most enchanting ways to Perpignan, but it is more than that: it is also a journey on which to linger, if you can, almost indefinitely. For the Corbières is the kind of region the discriminating traveller would like to keep to himself and a few kindred spirits; the kind of region in which historical and archaeological interest, so-called 'tourist facilities', transport networks and bargains in folklore fall into place as secondary stimuli compared with the ever-changing charm of the landscape. Mountainous without being grim, bathed in the golden southern light, it is fragrant with herbs and wild flowers.

This region of modest but none the less dramatic mountains and valleys (the highest peak, Bugarach, is about 1130 m/3700 ft) is bounded by the Pyrenees to the south, the River Aude to the west and north, and the Mediterranean (Barcarès-Leucate-Port-la-Novelle) to the east. It is one of the most distinctive areas of southern France and is particularly rich in the superbly situated ruins of ancient fortresses. These castles – the 'sons of Carcass-onne' – not only recall the Corbières' former role as Languedoc's last defence against Roussillon and the Spanish, but are also tragically rich in reminders of the fate of the Cathars in the medieval persecutions of religious dissidents.

The richness of the landscape itself, which forms the link between the Massif Central and the Pyrenees, lies in the mixture of magnificently wooded slopes, rugged and thyme-scented moor-land, masses of green broom and thorny gorse, oak and cypress, and mile after mile of vineyards. In the south the Gorges de Galamus are full of scenic drama, and in the east, not far from Perpignan, is the incredible fortress of Salses, an apparently indestructible mass of rose-, ochre- and sand-coloured brick and stone.

But the charm of the Corbières still lies more in its comparatively unknown corners and villages than in its history-laden relics, though even these have the advantage of having been less trumpeted abroad than the key sites of other areas of the south. Finding the best of the Corbières takes time, but the reward is joy in the region itself. This is particularly true if you are spending your holiday on the nearby coast, which, sun-baked, and well

Roussillon

provided for as it is, needs to be complemented with the wooded hills, sudden massifs, vine-clad valleys and unexpected villages of the hinterland. You need to explore on the spot to find Treilles, Feuilla, Opoul, Tautavel and other corners, but they are worth the effort. Leave the N9 (Narbonne to Perpignan) and turn off westwards along the kind of by-roads you thought no longer existed. And do not miss Lagrasse – where the D3 from Carcassone joins the D212 from Fabrezan, you get an excellent view of this village that is built like a strongpoint as the road descends. Lagrasse, with its 12th-century bridge and remains of ramparts, quiet central *place* and old houses, enshrines much of the special quality of the Corbières. Carcassone and Narbonne are approximately equidistant, each roughly 40 km (25 miles).

The Galamus Gorges
34 km (21 miles) from Quillan by the D117, or 41 km (25½ miles) from Perpignan is St Paul-de-Fenouillet. From here the D7 climbs up, casting views back towards the Roussillon countryside and the peaks of the Pyrenees Orientales, to the Gorges de Galamus, an impressive and wild fissure through the rock of the Corbières. From the viewpoint a track leads through the wooded slopes to the hermitage opposite. From here you get the full impact of the gorge with the green waters of the river just visible below. The hermitage, where once a hermit lived in a small hollow in the rock, now functions principally as a restaurant(or more properly a snackbar, considering the limited menu)-cum-hostel. From the gorge the road runs through countryside that opens out into pasture and vineyards enclosed in wide valleys by limestone knolls on top of which are perched the ruins of the 'sons of Carcassonne'.

Château de Peyrepertuse
Peyrepertuse is reached from Galamus by taking the D14 after Cubières and following this for 14 km (9 miles) to the other side of Duilhac. Here a road to the left takes you up the south side of the crest to the car park. Try to take the car as far as possible as there is still a fair walk round the crest and up to its summit to reach the château.

Around the château the country changes once more, the gorse and moorland of the Corbières becoming more apparent and the height of the limestone crests increasing so that the approach to the château and the château itself give majestic views towards Quéribus and east over the Corbières towards the sea. This splendid site has been occupied since Roman times, and in fact bears the remains of two medieval forts: the Château Bas and above, at the west end, the Château St George from where the marvellous view is found.

Below in the village of Duilhac, there is the very friendly Auberge du Vieux Moulin (tel 68 45 47 12) which provides generous helpings of good food at very modest prices. Beds are also available.

Château de Quéribus
7 km (4½ miles) further on from Duilhac, by the D14 then 123, is the Château de Quéribus. Built on the frontier between France and Aragon on a site chosen for its command of the Roussillon Plain, Quéribus was the final place of resistance by the Cathars. Their doomed stand of 1255 ended the Albigensian Crusades.

As with Peyrepertuse the final approach to the château has to be on foot, but the climb is well worth the effort for the breathtaking views south and east encompassing the Mediterranean, the plains of Roussillon, the Canigou Massif and the Pyrénées-Orientales. A complete panorama of the area is provided by the Grau de Maury, the shoulder of the pass (D123) below the château. The D123 now becomes the D19 and takes you to the village of Maury and back to the D117 for Perpignan. The entire loop from St Paul to Maury is only 37 km (23 miles) or so but what with the size of the roads and the time needed to enjoy the sites, a good half day is needed to do the area justice.

Abbaye de Fontfroide
Fontfroide is accessible from the D613 which connects with the N113 from Carcassonne to Narbonne, joining it roughly 5 km (3 miles) from the latter.

The abbey contains one of the most beautiful cloisters (with exquisite marble columns) in southern France. Founded at the end of the 11th century by the Cistercian Order, Fontfroide has been in private hands since 1908 and has been restored with taste and care. The abbey is in a well-kept setting of gardens and walks bordering the River Gue. Visits are possible during most of the year, the tours lasting about half an hour. (There is a moderate charge.)

Fort-de-Salses
Built to last in 1497 by Ferdinand D'Aragon but altered by Vauban in l691, shortly after Roussillon fell to the French for the last time, the outer walls are 9 m (30 ft) thick in parts and equipped with a huge number of firing posts, which made the fortress invulner-

able to the short-range cannon-fire of its day. But it is not merely the brooding size and ominous closed face of Salses that creates its unique impression among the most ancient fortresses of France: the sight of its red, russet and ochre walls, Spanish towers and great gateway in the Mediterranean light is both beautiful and haunting.

Regional Wines
The small town of Salses produces delicious white wines called Macabeu (pronounced Macabeou) that are reminiscent of the Portuguese *vinho verde*. However, the principal wines of the area are the heavy red wines of the Corbières which are rich in strength and colour, with a bouquet which recalls the herb-scented *garrigue*: delicious, and a little goes a long way. A wine of more subtlety, and the only Corbières wine of *appellation*-rank, is the Fitou originating a few miles north of Salses. Bordering the D118 between Carcassonne and Quillan is the vine-growing area known as the Blanquette de Limoux producing a very palatable, sparkling wine and a *mousseux* dessert wine.

Roussillon wines are again predominantly red, the main labels being Côte de Roussillon and Côte de Roussillon-Villages, both very drinkable and on the way up. Between Roussillon and the Corbières, there are some 400,000 acres of vineyard accounting for a third of France's total wine production.

Perpignan

Perpignan is in some ways the most exotic town in the south of France. The charm of the other cities in the sun comes from a mixture of reminders of the antique world, the enclosed nature of medievalism, the French village *place* with its trees and soft-coloured walls and midday balm. Perpignan is different. It has most of the qualities of the other towns, but with an additional flavour, an extra dimension. The main impression conveys more of Spain and North Africa than of Rome or the Franks, a Spanish-Arab mixture of intense heat, intense colour and intensely black shadow.

Time was when one discovered Perpignan on the way to Collioure or Banyuls, or because one had caught a glimpse of the magic Roussillon. Recently it has become the last chance for motorists to fill up with French milk and honey before heading for the oil and *paella* of the popular Spanish coastal resorts. It can be overcrowded with transit traffic and unbearably hot in the eye of August, but its ageless qualities make it uniquely fascinating.

The Syndicat d'Initiative (tel 68 34 13 13) is in the Palais des Congrès. Alternatively, and somewhat better, is the regional office, the Comité Départmental de Tourisme de Pyrénées-Roussillon (tel 68 34 29 94), in the Quai de Lattre-de-Tassigny. This will dispense information on accommodation, restaurants, camping, sights etc. both in Perpignan and Roussillon as a whole.

Palace of the Kings of Majorca

In the first edition of this guide, Maurice Rosenbaum wrote: 'It is about forty years since I first wandered by chance through a short tunnel in the earthworks near the local barracks and ancient citadel and found myself in the incredible courtyards of the Palace of the Kings of Majorca. The restoration of this splendid survival had, in fact, only just begun three years previously, and the impact was, perhaps, even greater then than it is on unprepared visitors today. This in spite of the glass pyramid that serves as a ticket office and the haunting piped music on endless repeat that seem, with the Palace and distant mountains, to belong to the realms of fantasy.'

Historically, the site is of considerable interest in the tangled story of the separation and demarcation of nations. Roussillon, which in the 2nd century BC was part of the great Roman province of the Narbonnaise, became, after invasions by Visigoths and Arabs, a bone of contention between France and Spain. Pepin the Short wrested it from the Arabs in the 8th century and subjected it to the Count of Barcelona. It was handed over, by the last hereditary Count, to the King of Aragon in 1172. In the 13th century, Jacques I of Aragon, who had captured the Balearic Islands from the Muslims, made a gift of them to his son, along with Roussillon, Cerdagne and Montpellier. The son took the title of King of Majorca and made Perpignan his capital. In 1344, after three kings of Majorca had reigned, Pierre IV of Aragon took over what was left of their territories.

But in spite of the extraordinary history of the palace, here again, as in so many parts of southern France, a visit is recommended for the interest and beauty of the building itself rather than for its historical importance. For most holidaymakers an attempt to associate the places they visit with remote and unfamiliar historical episodes is more exhausting than enjoyable. Only if one comes across a site that suddenly brings to life a fragment of history or literature which one has always found absorbing does the story behind it become as exciting as the spectacle itself. Most times it is better to respond simply to the thing in itself – the building, the panorama and so on – to its visual charm or interest, or merely to the fact that you came across it on a fine day when all was going well.

The Palace of the Kings of Majorca is very much a thing in itself, a splendid example of royal architecture of the 13th and 14th centuries, with a magnificent square courtyard flanked by a double gallery with a series of arcades. Entry to the courtyard is through great arches, which themselves support an elegant loggia of six Gothic arcades from the second half of the 14th century. At the far end of the courtyard the 'Paradise' gallery is supported by the wide arches of the lower gallery, and other arcades, Romanesque and Gothic, add to the elegance of the whole structure. The Gothic elements, particularly in the arcaded bell-tower, are comparatively rare in the Roussillon of that period.

Le Castillet
On the south side of the Place de la Victoire stands Le Castillet, a fortress in dark red brick that gives a Spanish-African flavour to the heart of the city. From the top of the fortress, 142 steps high, there is a fine view over the Loge de Mer to the Roussillon Plain and mountains and in the other direction towards the Mediterranean. Le Castillet also contains, in the Casa Pairal, a museum of Catalan arts and folklore. The fortress is open all week (except Tuesday) and entry is free.

La Loge de Mer
Dating from the 14th to 16th centuries, the Loge was created originally to house a finance market or exchange (*bourse*) and a sea consulate or *tribunal de commerce maritime*. It forms part of a complex of buildings ranging from the 13th to 16th centuries which includes the old Palais de Justice and Hôtel de Ville. Opposite this complex, across the Place de la Loge, runs the small Rue des Fabriques d'En Nabot. Roughly halfway down, at the first intersection, is the Maison Julia, one of the best preserved *hôtels particuliers* of Perpignan, with charming Gothic balconies dating from the 14th century.

St Jean Cathedral
Although building was started in 1324 by the second King of Majorca, the cathedral was not consecrated until 1509. However, the work of most interest is a wooden sculpture of Christ found in the small side chapel on the south side of the cathedral.

Accommodation and Restaurants
Of Perpignan's 3-star hotels the Hôtel de Loge (tel 68 34 54 84) and the Mas des Arcades (tel 68 85 11 11) are well recommended.

The latter is found 2 km (1 mile) south of the centre on the N9 and offers both swimming and tennis. 2-star hotels include the Hôtel Kennedy (tel 68 50 60 02) and, more centrally in Rue Queya, the Athéna (tel 68 34 37 63). Neither have a restaurant. In the 1-star bracket but well located, being near Le Castillet and just around the corner from a whole range of restaurants, is the Bristol (tel 68 34 32 68) in the Rue Grande des Fabriques. The youth hostel (tel 68 34 63 32) is found just off the Avenue de Grande-Bretagne which runs parallel to the River Têt to the north-west of the city centre.

The area around Place de la Loge, immediately south of Le Castillet, is well supplied with affordable restaurants, and the Loge de Mer itself has been converted into a hamburger joint. A little to the west, along the Quai Vauban, are more expensive places overlooking the canal. Otherwise the Delcros in Avenue M. Leclerc is recommended.

St Michel-de-Cuxa

This marvellous abbey lies roughly 45 km (28 miles) south-west of Perpignan by the N116 to Prades. 2 km (1 mile) further on (D27) the abbey's crenellated tower battles with the Canigou Massif behind for domination of the valley.

The abbey's history is convoluted. Consecrated in 974, the original building was aggrandized in the 11th century and entered a period of prosperity ending with the inevitable collapse and sale of all its treasures during the Revolution. The cloisters were also dismantled for their beautifully carved capitals and it was not until 1907 that the first attempts to reassemble the columns were made by the American sculptor George Grey Barnard. They were then bought by a New York museum in 1925 and were finally reassembled in Fort Tryon Park overlooking the Hudson River. Since 1952 the abbey itself has been restored, along with the remaining cloisters, and there are once more monks in residence.

Despite their incompleteness the cloisters are well worth seeing for the 12th-century capitals which are distinguished by their lack of religious motifs. Otherwise wander around the outside of the abbey past the field devoted to iris breeding by the monks for a spectacular view of the abbey's tower against the Canigou Massif. A walk through the vineyards on the other side of the abbey brings equally fine views as the path rises into the woods.

Prades

Prades unfortunately has little that would attract the tourist. Unfortunately because it was in Prades that the medieval manuscripts were found that gave rise to the Montaillou story – Emmanuel le Roy Laduvie's account of life in a 14th-century village.

If you intend staying in the area it is worth travelling a few miles to the north-west along the D14 to Moltig-les-Bains where you will find the superb Château Hôtel de Riell (tel 68 05 04 40). Open from April to the start of November, this 4-star hotel has sports facilities and an excellent restaurant. The 3-star Grand Hôtel Thermal (tel 69 05 00 50) is good, quiet and also offers tennis and swimming, being open over a similar time period to the Château. The baths in Moltig are supposed to be beneficial for skin and respiratory ailments.

Le Prieure de Serrabonne

15 km (9 miles) from Prades, back along the N116 to Perpignan, take the turning to the right to Bouleternere, and follow the D618 for approximately 8 km (5 miles) until the turn off for the priory – 4 km (2½ miles) of hairpin bends away. At first sight from the approach road the priory looks unremarkable, being constructed of unrelieved schist. However, once through the entrance and into the South Gallery dating from the 12th century, one is immediately attracted to the columns and the various beasts that constitute their capitals and the backdrop of the valley and the forested Aspres hills. But the showpiece of the priory is found inside the form of the tribune. Again in the Romanesque style, the richness of the carvings depicting mythological beasts, lions and eagles is breathtaking. Serrabonne is closed on Tuesdays.

If you have time for a fairly long country drive, on leaving the priory continue along the D618 through the Aspres hills and such charming villages as Boule-d'Amont, almost lost behind bends in the road. Though little more than a hamlet, Boule-d'Amont has a good if slightly expensive *auberge*. Perhaps of less interest but noteworthy all the same is its church which still retains its original 10th-century door complete with ironwork.

5 km (3 miles) after Boule comes a crossroad on the Col Fourtou. To stay on the D618 one has to take the left-hand turn. For the next 20 km (12½ miles) the road travels through the practically untouched heart of the Aspres with tranquil views of the wooded slopes of neighbouring ranges of hills and mountains stretching

south towards the Roc de France that marks the border with Spain. The Château de Belpuig, above the village of De la Trinité, in return for a half-hour walk to reach it, gives an impressive panorama of these mountains from the Corbières to the Albères and the Canigou Massif. Eventually, after a sharp bend, the road descends from the Col Xalada into the Tech Valley and the attractively sited spa town of Amélie-les-Bains. From here the D115 and N9 will take you the 38 km (24 miles) back to Perpignan.

Canet-en-Roussillon

Formerly simply Canet-Plage, this coastal town, only 13 km (8 miles) from Perpignan and consequently very much the city's beach, is now the grandly re-titled holiday complex Canet-en-Roussillon St Nazaire with a vast beach 9 km (5½ miles) long and 100 m (328 ft) wide shelving gently into the sea. A pleasure port with over 750 berths, there is every conceivable facility for sport and exercise, games and gambling. It is also well equipped with hotels, flats, villas and studios and, if all this is not enough (or too much) there is a quiet, pleasant hinterland.

Collioure and the Côte Vermeille

Collioure, in spite of rapid expansion – it is still officially credited with only 2750 offical inhabitants – remains one of the most picturesque fishing ports of the whole French Mediterranean coast from Cerbère to Menton. It consists, in fact, of two small ports, separated by the huge mass of the 12th-century Templars' castle, the Château Royale, which is placed pictorially – seen from the sea – next to the tough-looking 17th-century church of St Vincent. The church itself, with its feet in the water, is built on to an old lighthouse converted into a clock-tower with a charming pink cupola. Between the castle and the church the beach is bordered by fishing boats carrying in their bows the great lamps still used for fishing *au lamparo* at night. Behind the church lie the narrow streets and alleys of the old town (the Quartier du Mouré). The SI (tel 68 82 15 47) in the Place de la Mairie, is a good source of local information on accommodation, sights and so on.

Beyond St Vincent is a small island of the same name from whose tiny chapel the length of the Côte Vermeille can be seen. A stunning coastal walk also runs from the ancient Château St Vincent. Allow up to an hour.

Collioure shares with Cêret an honoured place in the history of modern painting and was much favoured by Matisse, Derain,

Roussillon

Dufy, Juan Gris, Picasso and many others whose works can be seen in the Musée de Collioure on the Port Vendres road. The Château Royale, which attained its present form through the fortifications of Vauban in the 17th century, also houses displays of contemporary art and local history. Vauban was also responsible for the now ruined towers that once watched over Collioure from the Albères hills behind.

Accommodation and Restaurants
Being a popular resort, hotels are expensive. Of the 3-star establishments the Casa Pairal (tel 68 82 05 81), an attractive place with pool and garden, is probably your best bet. Les Templiers (tel 68 82 05 58) has a collection of paintings left as gifts or as payment by the many artists that have passed through or stayed in Collioure. Restaurants represent a difficult choice, there always being one that looks better just round the corner. This is particularly true of the Quartier du Mouré which is full of small intimate *tapas* bars and the like.

Hermitage of Notre Dame de Consolation

Do not miss a trip to the Hermitage if only for the views over the terraced vineyards to Collioure and back up the coast towards Perpignan. Take the N114 from Collioure in the direction of Argelès. About a kilometre out of town at the top of the first slope, turn left on to the D86 and follow this for just over 3 km (2 miles) until, at a crossroads, an old sign directs you left down to the site. Beyond the rather seedy-looking café lies the chapel and, in a courtyard beyond that, under the shade of the plane trees, are set out lines of stone picnic tables. It is here that the locals congregate for their Sunday lunches with family and friends, carting up crates of wine, seafood and mineral water, all cooled by boxes of ice. The tables can be hired from the café. From the courtyard a path runs uphill through abandoned groves and by a small crumbling aqueduct to a natural spring that now bypasses the temple-like fountain built for it.

Further along the D86, which ends in Banyuls-sur-Mer, 20 km (12½ miles) from Collioure, is the Tour Madeloc, which gives excellent views over the Côte Vermeille and Roussillon. The tower dates from the time of the Kings of Aragon and Majorca.

Port Vendres

About 3 km (2 miles) from Collioure towards the Spanish frontier is Port Vendres, a small port for passenger and car-ferry services to Algeria and Morocco. It is also an active fishing centre and there is a marina and a beach nearby with good bathing. The passenger port is a small rectangular basin in which a delightful way of spending time can be to sit on the terrace of a waterfront café and watch some of the bigger ships berth with literally inches to spare. Although the name means 'Port of Venus' the cult of Venus does not seem to be any more insistent here than anywhere else along the coast. Unfortunately the outskirts of the town are largely ugly modern villas and flats and much of Port Vendres seems to be little more than an overflow from Collioure.

Banyuls-sur-Mer

Banyuls-sur-Mer, about 7 km (4½ miles) nearer Spain by the N114, prides itself on being the most southerly holiday resort of France's Mediterranean coast. It was also the birthplace of the great sculptor Aristide Maillot (1861–1944) and the home of Banyuls, a full-bodied slightly sweet wine – sometimes compared with port – grown on the nearby slopes which are terraced with dry-stone walls. Banyuls' other point of interest is the aquarium, just off the main road, where specimens of the rich local marine fauna can be seen. Indeed so rich are the waters in this area that a reserve has been established between Banyuls and Cerbère, and Banyuls is also home to a marine laboratory, part of the University of Paris.

All in all Banyuls is, and has long been, an excellent family holiday centre, at the heart of the Côte Vermeille, with every type of sport and recreation within reach, 12 km (7½ miles) of bays and creeks, a pleasant Catalan hinterland, and an excellent choice of hotels, such as the 3-star Hôtel Le Catalan (tel 68 88 02 80) which has every amenity including tennis and swimming plus a good view of the town and sea. Flats, studios and campsites, of which the Syndicat d'Initiative (tel 68 88 31 58) in Avenue République can give details, are also available.

Cerbère

The French Mediterranean coast ends 10 km (6 miles) further on at Cerbère, basically a small fishing port in an inlet sheltered to the north by Cap Canadell and to the south by Cap Cerbère, it is a pleasant spot despite a railway viaduct. There is a small marina and a good sandy beach, hotels, pensions and camping. The SI (tel 68 88 41 49) is open only from July to mid-September.

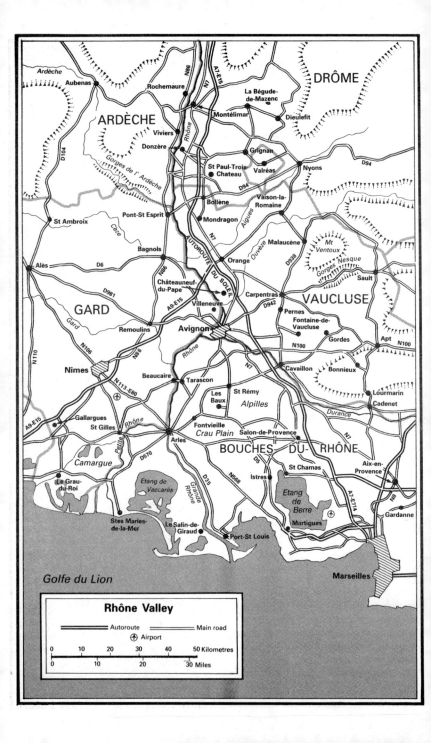

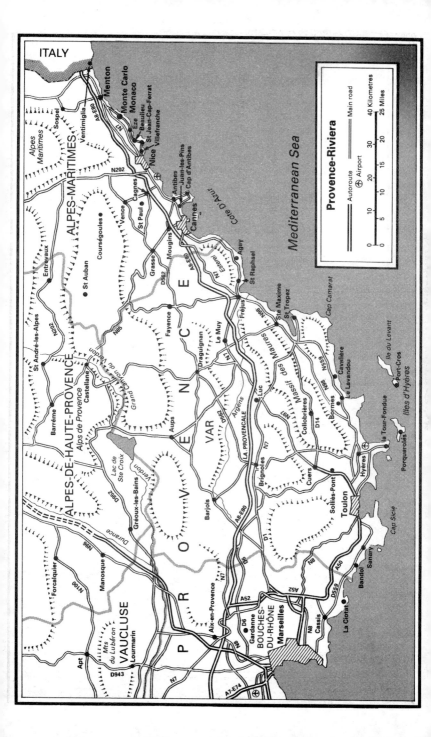

Provence-Riviera

Autoroute   Main road

⊕ Airport

0   10   20   30   40 Kilometres
0   5   10   15   20   25 Miles

ITALY

Menton
Monte Carlo
Monaco
Ventimiglia
Sospel
Èze
Beaulieu
St-Jean-Cap-Ferrat
Nice
Villefranche
Alpes Maritimes
Entrevaux
St Auban
Courségoules
Vence
St Paul
Cagnes
Antibes
Juan-les-Pins
Cap d'Antibes
Cannes
Grasse
Mougins
Côte D'Azur

ALPES-MARITIMES

St André-les-Alpes
Castellane
Fayence
Agay
St Raphaël
Draguignan
Le Muy
Fréjus
Ste Maxime
St Tropez
Cap Camarat

Barrême
Aups
Lac de Ste Croix
Gréoux-les-Bains
Barjols
Luc
Collobrières
Cavalière
Le Lavandou
Îles d'Hyères
Île du Levant
Port-Cros

ALPES-DE-HAUTE-PROVENCE
Alps de Provence
Verdon
Grand Canon du Verdon
Durance

Brignoles
Cuers
Solliès-Pont
Bormes
Hyères
La Tour-Fondue
Porquerolles
Cap Sicié

Forcalquier
Manosque
Mts du Lubéron
Apt
Lourmarin

VAUCLUSE

Aix-en-Provence
Gardanne
Marseilles
Cassis
La Ciotat
Bandol
Sanary
Toulon

BOUCHES-DU-RHÔNE

PROVENCE
VAR

Mediterranean Sea

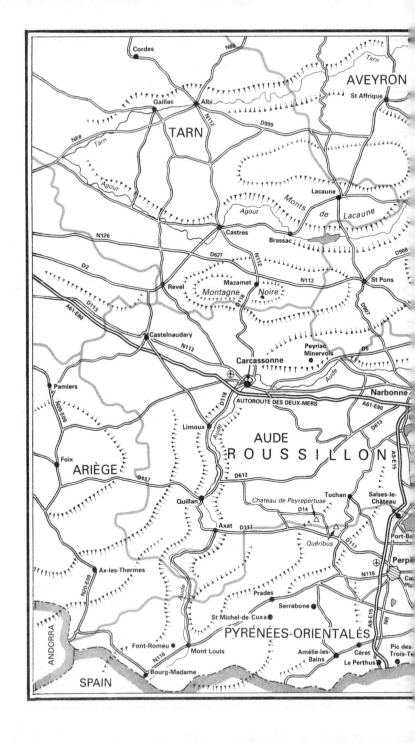

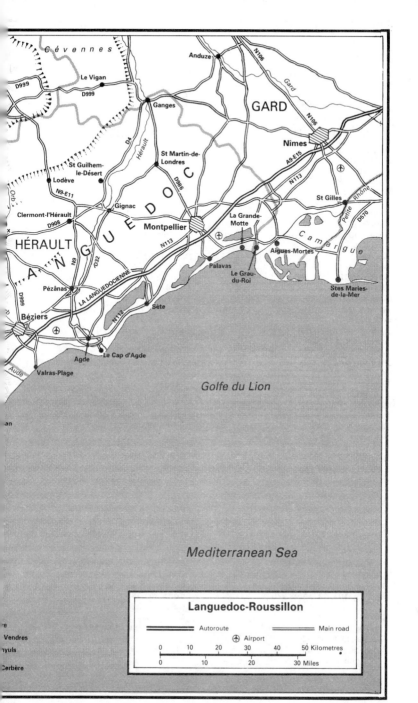

Index

Page references to photographs appear in **bold** type